Acknowledgments

I want to express my undying love and appreciation to my ever patient and loving husband, Len, and my wonderful children, Matthew and Elizabeth, for putting up with me during the most intense times with the "Girls" and supporting me in all the craziness that seems to follow me. I could not have done any of this without their love and support.

I owe a huge debt of gratitude to my Pastor, Rev. Brian Spencer, who, for the past 19 years, has encouraged and discipled me, accepted me for who I am, and appreciated those gifts that others have found, at times, offensive. He has taught me much about "erring on the side of grace".

To Nancy Dorner who has taken me under her wing and taught me so much about writing and ministry and most importantly about prayer and obedience, thank you for your inexhaustible encouragement and wisdom and your prayers.

To Sherry Rial, my heartfelt thanks for your friendship, encouragement, your professional insights, and for letting me drag you into so many things.

To Kathie Dawn, because I said I would and I keep my promises.

And last but certainly not least, I can never adequately express my thanks and deep appreciation for my sisters in Christ whose lives inspired this work. You are my heroes.

DEDICATED IN LOVING MEMORY OF MY DAD

Reverend L. LaVail Maguire
1921-1993

Who lived what he believed

"For me to live is Christ, to die is gain."
Philippians 1:21

Table of Contents

INTRODUCTION

In today's society, some say that there are worse things than death and after reading the accounts of the women in this book, you may at first be inclined to agree. But within these pages you will find the heart beat of hope. Steady, strong, and vital.

The statistics within the church today on divorce, and the devastation that sexual immorality is having on our homes and families are appalling. But even more disturbing is the response of believers to these unsettling statistics. Women everywhere seem to have a fatalistic complacency in their lives. They are buying the lie that relationships do not last and cannot be healed and are giving up on their marriages and, more importantly, on God. Women in these situations have many resources to turn to but there are too few actual true-life success stories available to women at large to encourage and give women hope that God truly does care and work in their lives. In their darkest moments, that is what the women you will meet within these pages craved, and they've committed to God to share their stories to give others a glimpse of God's light in those darkest moments.

My prayer is that you will find a consistent, prevailing thread throughout these pages proving that God is still in control, that He never changes, and that He still cares and is all powerful in our lives even through seemingly impossible circumstances.

This is simply the true story of ordinary women with extraordinary stories of faith, struggle, pain, sisterhood, accountability, and God's sovereign grace in bringing us all together to form what we have come to call ourselves, The 1st Peter 3 girls.

CHAPTER ONE

Lori

Some say that there are worse things than death...

I met Dan early in 1980. It was the New Year and my husband Len and I had decided to work in volunteer youth ministry and were going through our local Youth for Christ's associate staff training program. Dan, just out of high school, was also enrolled in the training classes. He was shy but very likable. And being a newlywed with a mother-hen complex I immediately "adopted" Dan. We were living in a basement apartment and eventually the upstairs of the home would be occupied by three women friends, one of whom was Sherry, our ministry supervisor at YFC. Dan had quickly become a regular fixture in our home and with the friends we spent time with. We were having lots of fun at the house back then with Bible studies, fellowships and just hanging out, sometimes all night. We were young and immature but growing in our faith and sharing experiences.

It was obvious that Dan didn't seem to share a lot of himself with us but we attributed this to his personality and shyness. He was just there, enjoying the company and many times chauffeuring the "gang" places since he was the only one with a cool car, a brand new yellow Chevette. A little cramped but what fun memories.

1

Over the years Dan would begin to share a little more of himself with Sherry or myself at times, but not often. Thinking that he just needed to meet the "right girl" our goal, for a time, became to "fix Dan up" with a nice Christian girl and try to get him to come out of his shell, but with no apparent success.

The years seemed to pass quickly. Len and I moved and started a family and one by one the girls upstairs and the rest of our "gang" either went on to graduate from college or got married and we all moved on to the next phase in our lives. Dan went on to attend a university out of town, but kept in touch. When he was home he would still come over and just hang out or we would get together with some of the old gang but he was becoming increasingly distant. I knew from talking with him that he had gotten out of the habit of attending church and was compromising on friendships at school but kept trying to encourage him in his walk with the Lord.

It eventually became evident that things were not going well for Dan spiritually. Doing poorly in school he changed universities and moved back to the area. He wasn't in church at all and he began calling every month or so to "confess" his sins of partying and bad relationship choices. It broke my heart to talk to him. We would both end up in tears. It was like watching my own brother throwing his life away.

I am not sure what triggered what seemed to be a turn around for Dan, but he began attending church again and appeared to be getting his life back on track. We were thrilled. He was attending our church and getting involved. At this same time a co-worker of Dan's set him up on a blind date. It turned out to be someone he knew and had gone to high school with. They began dating and he called to tell me about her.

My first question was "Is she a Christian?". He didn't hesitate and came back with a "Yes". I was relieved; things seemed to be rolling along for Dan down a positive godly path. He told us that she was divorced and had two small children and had come to know the Lord after her first husband had left her for another woman. I was curious and, of course, wanted to meet her. I didn't have to wait long. It was only a couple of months later when Dan called, "I think I'm going to marry her".

I was stunned; he had gone from asking questions about Christians and divorce to buying an engagement ring inside of two months while not sharing much at all about how he felt. I was really curious now and of course concerned for my friend. He called and wanted to bring her over in December of 1989 so we set up a time to get together.

I really didn't know what to expect since Dan hadn't told us much detail about Lori but I was pleasantly surprised. She was pretty, and friendly, but what struck me most was her directness and boldness in talking about the Lord. She was a babe in Christ. She had only known the Lord for about a year and divorced a little more than that but you could tell her conversion was genuine and her attitude very open. At one point, when the men had left the room, she turned and looked me straight in the eye and said, "So, Dan says you know him better than anybody, can you tell me honestly if you think he is ready to make this commitment and can I trust him?"

Marlene Lawson

That was a fair question after what she had already been through. This woman wanted to do what God wanted her to and her honesty and directness humbled me. I answered her as best I could. I told her from what I had seen in Dan's spiritual growth and what he had been through that if he was willing to make this commitment then "yes" I felt he was ready and could be trusted.

As I look back on that moment now I feel a certain amount of responsibility for some of what happened over the next several months and years. I have a much greater caution in answering questions like that one and know that I failed Dan and Lori both by not spending critical time in prayer for my friends. At the same time, I know God is sovereign and in control and Lori had prayed about their relationship and felt that God wanted her to marry Dan.

Lori had come through a very painful, traumatic, divorce. Having had her first husband leave her while she was pregnant for their second child, she, as a new Christian, was looking for a godly man to be a father to her two very young children, and I did not see the red flags and warning signals in Dan's life. The sad thing is that Dan considered Len and I his closest friends and as it turned out, we did not even know who Dan was.

Lori was expecting life with a Christian man to be, if not perfect, at least normal and different than being married to a non-Christian. Marriage to Dan turned out to be certainly different. She sensed something was not quite right even as early as their honeymoon but could not put her finger on it.

Lori and I developed a close discipleship relationship during the months since we had met and we talked frequently. She was growing in her walk with the Lord but was becoming increasingly concerned about their marriage relationship. He was uncommunicative and distant and did not seem to want to participate in any type of intimacy. He was becoming more and more depressed and estranged. She, in turn, was beginning to question her own expectations of marriage and God's direction in her life and was becoming frustrated. It took two years, a series of difficult circumstances and stress, and the birth of their daughter, to bring Dan to the point of revealing what he had been hiding from everyone in his life for over 20 years.

On a Friday morning some two years after their marriage, Lori called me in tears. Dan had gone to work and left her a letter confessing for the first time what he had been struggling with most of his life. When I arrived at their home, Lori, still in tears and without a word, handed me the letter. As I read it my heart began to break and I was devastated. I had had no idea. I was stunned. It seemed Dan had been living a double life. In the letter he informed Lori that he had been struggling with homosexuality since adolescence. The wording of the letter seemed to blame God and was hopelessly fatalistic. He couldn't change. He had tried. He was miserable and depressed and didn't know what to do.

This was just the beginning of the long road that God was asking Lori, Dan, Len and myself to travel together. It was also the just the beginning of the confessions. We would soon learn that Dan also had an addiction to pornography and was deeply in bondage. Dan had wrongly assumed that by marrying and putting on the façade of a "normal" life his sin would go away. He thought if he jumped through the hoops and looked and acted like a "normal" Christian then all the bondage, guilt, shame and turmoil would simply disappear.

At this point I would like to say that I believe that there is no such thing as a "normal" Christian and that our lives cannot be based upon what today's religious society has deemed "normal". The standard has always been, and will always be Jesus Christ and Him alone. It is a much higher calling and standard than any outward form, habit or tradition man has set. Satan is the father of lies and would continue to lie and deceive Dan for six more years before he would understand God's grace and forgiveness and the power that comes from the Holy Spirit to overcome sin. And in the mean time God would take Lori and I on a very intense and painful journey learning about God's grace and forgiveness in her own life as well.

The following days and weeks after Dan's confession were an emotional roller coaster. How do we respond? What do we say? How do we love and restore, yet stand firm on the very clear principles in God's Word regarding Dan's specific sins and how it had affected all of us? It soon became apparent that Dan had "confessed" but had not taken any steps toward true repentance. At first he seemed very relieved to have it out in the open, almost giddy. But it didn't take long before he began to, once again, retreat emotionally and manipulate people around him to blame and save face.

He would say what was expected and make attempts to participate in the relationship but then would seem to withdraw into a robot type shell. He became very mechanical. Lori thought she was being loving and accepting, trying to help him heal. She would initiate conversation about their relationship. Discussing, *she* thought, goals they both wanted for intimacy and communication. Dan would seem to agree without actually making any verbal commitments. She would do most of the talking thinking that his passive acceptance was agreement. He would say he didn't know how and ask 'what did she want him to do?' And Lori would, of course, make it easy for him and describe what she thought a Godly husband and intimate marriage involved. Dan would, in turn, go through the motions of "doing" what Lori had told him a good husband does, again, in a very passive manner. This would last for a week or two and then he would again retreat into a sullen, almost catatonic like state. Lori would then try to talk to him and draw him out of his shell but he would become angry and twist her words, and it would end up being "her fault". This cycle would continue to repeat itself and as Lori would ask him questions, he would lie and tell her what he thought she wanted to hear until it would blow up again and he would "confess" and tell her what he had really been doing. She would be terribly hurt and wounded and we were all very frustrated and didn't know where to turn.

Lori went to our pastor and his wife for counsel and advice and they referred them to a very Biblically sound counselor. Dan agreed to go to the counselor but, again, did not initiate his own "recovery". He did what he was told but would do nothing without being pushed. Lori needed daily encouragement and was struggling with her own role in all this. How do you respond to something like this? Should she leave him? Tell him to go get his act together and then he can come home? She also had the children to think about. They needed to be protected from this sin and the potential harm that could result.

What I respect about Lori is her desire to do what God wants, not just what seems right at the time. Even as a babe in Christ, she did not turn tail and run, nor did she do anything rash out of panic. We began to pray for direction and for God's leading.

As Lori and I spent time together trying to make sense of her devastating situation we began to look at scripture to find answers in the midst of all the pain. I had been privileged enough to have been raised in a pastors home where the power of God was not only preached, but lived. I knew what God could do and I knew there had to be answers for Lori and direction in the middle of chaos. God would give Lori strength and patiently and lovingly take her through the darkest days of her life and sustain her by giving her sisters to lean on. He would teach us both about the Body of Christ. About accountability. About faith and trust in Christ who loved us enough to die for us and suffer more than we could ever imagine

Lori and I didn't know it then, but our relationship would be the first in setting the stage for the ministry that was to take place in the lives of nine women that God would bring together that would eventually become the 1st Peter 3 girls.

CHAPTER TWO

"Where Do We Go From Here?"

Pain. Unbelievable emotional pain. Hopelessness. Frustration. Feelings of helplessness and failure. Lori was feeling all of these things. And I was feeling it right along with her, along with the guilt of wondering if there was anything I could have done to prevent this or help Dan. Now it wasn't just Dan's life that was a mess, it had affected Lori, three innocent, unsuspecting children, extended family, and yes, even the church family. The implications were huge. Even though most of these other people didn't know what was going on, it *did* affect them. In 1 Corinthians 5 Paul addresses moral sins in the church at Corinth. 1Cor. 5:6b *"...Don't you know that a little yeast works through the whole batch of dough?" NIV*

Christians today are buying into Satan's lie that what I do in the privacy of my own home is my business. No one needs to know I have this struggle. I can handle it. It's not hurting anyone else.

We forget the very character of God. He cannot even look upon sin *of any kind.* No one else may know our hearts but God does. And as our loving heavenly Father he *must*, because of His character, deal with sin in our lives. We are His children to love, grow and discipline. And often, when we are willful, the discipline is painful.

Hebrews 12:6 "because the Lord disciplines those he loves, and he punishes everyone who he accepts as a son." NIV

9

Discipline isn't always pleasant, and this definitely would get worse before it would get better.

I knew, by this time, some of the circumstances and choices Dan had made early on in adolescence that started him on the path that had brought him to this point. Our pastor often says that each of us has full freedom over the choices we make but we do not have freedom over the results of those choices. It was painfully clear how Dan got here.

But what about Lori?

She had to address all the unanswered questions bombarding her spirit. Why her? She was a fairly new believer. Why, now? She didn't deserve this. These were not the consequences of *her* choices. She had been lied to and deceived. Didn't she have a right to walk away? Just dump the baggage and start over?

Lori began receiving a lot of interesting advise from other Christians who became aware of their situation. Lori was looking for Biblical answers and direction and approached several people for "godly" counsel. She was given a myriad of advice. She was told to do everything from;

"Get out now and protect yourself and the kids before it's too late"

To,

"Become a 'fascinating woman' and then God will make Dan the man you want him to be",

To,

"Just initiate and be aggressive in the relationship if he won't do it",

To,

"This is such a huge sin problem that there is little hope of Dan ever really successfully dealing with it or of you ever having a normal, intimate marriage so either get out now or resign yourself to it".

As the circle of people who knew became larger, most shook their heads, "tisk tisked" and turned the other way. No one wanted to deal with this one.

I was becoming angry as I heard much of the so-called "advice" she was getting. I am no counselor, and don't have any easy answers, but I *do* know the Mighty Counselor and Prince of Peace who does and Lori and I turned to Scripture to find out what the Word had to say. Now don't get me wrong, I believe strongly that there is a significant place for Christian counselors today but many times we opt first to go to a counselor before we consult God's Word. And often the answers, while not easy, are right in front of us.

Both Lori and Dan were going to a Christian counselor together but, for the most part, the focus was to help Dan deal with his crisis and to try to help them both work on the marriage. Dan was getting a lot of attention and Lori was getting a lot of "advice". She was obviously having her own personal crisis and needed not only to seek Godly counsel from a professional, but on a daily basis, someone to come along side her and give her encouragement. Someone to help her to keep her eyes focused on Jesus and walk daily in the secure hand of God through the emotional land mines of the situation.

God's Word tells us that in the Body of Christ, God does not expect us to bear pain alone. Scripture teaches clearly that we are to love one another, bear with one another, bear one another's burdens, weep with one another, and so on. We have a responsibility to each other in the Body of Christ to actually get involved.

One of the things that I believe is prevalent in the Church in our society today, is that it appears that we no longer seem to know how to function as a body. God's Word says that the eye cannot say to the hand "I don't need you". Consequently we cannot say to a brother or sister in Christ "I feel bad about your pain but it doesn't concern me and I don't know how to help you", and then just walk away. When you hit your thumb with a hammer, or stub your toe on a rock, the entire body reacts. You can feel the pain throb all through your body to even the roots of your hair it seems. You may even visibly cringe, making the pain also obvious to others around you. There is a reason why Christ used the picture of a physical body to describe how the Church is to function. We are to be *relational* not traditional or superficial. Christ was relational. He cared about *people,* not what they looked like or where they went to church or whether they sang in the choir or wore a suit or even how much money they make or where they work. He wanted to heal their wounds and hurts and forgive their sins.

I also believe that, in today's society, Christians' view of God in general has shrunk dramatically. Just before the new millenium, I heard a gentleman speak on a Focus on the Family radio broadcast regarding the Y2k bug and his observation was that we as Christians in this society have more faith in science than we do in God. We are more likely to think God will fail than science and technology. How sad for us who call ourselves His children. We rob ourselves of the miracle of knowing the awesome Father God who created us. Our world has become so small and finite.

So, as we searched the Scriptures for answers, where did that leave us? Lori began to get a picture of who God really is and focus on that awesome God. The One who created all heaven and earth and each living thing. The One who parted the Red Sea. Shut the mouths of the lions. Who came down and lived among us and died and rose again to save us from our sins and an ultimate eternity in Hell. The bottom line Lori had to face was 'Is God really who He says He is?' and 'Is the Bible Truth?' Is it relevant even in a situation as horrible as the one she found herself in?

I remember saying those two things to Lori day after day. I'm sure she got sick of hearing it. No, I *know* she did. But each of us who call ourselves "Christian" need to address these fundamental questions because if He isn't then as Paul said, "we labor in vain". Cut your losses and get out now, which, unfortunately is the reaction most Christians seemed to have to Lori's situation.

Lori began to take God at his Word. We entered into an intense accountability/discipleship relationship. We did not make a conscious decision to do this, it was just understood. Lori, still in shock, needed to go over this time and again and needed to refocus daily on God and his Word. It was as if the earth beneath her was suddenly gone and she was hanging on for dear life to the only lifeline within her grasp.

We would talk regularly on the phone, usually each morning after Dan left for work. We would agree to pray specifically about each day asking for direction for Lori. What should she say and do? She needed prayer and encouragement each and every day to face the terrible reality of the situation and we both knew the Lord had placed us together in this. This was no overnight fix-it situation. Even if Dan, having confessed, did a total turn around it would take serious work to heal and repair lives. But Dan, having relieved the immediate pressure of guilt by confessing, stopped short of repentance. He was jumping through hoops again. He had changed clothes outwardly, so to speak, but not washed internally in the blood of Jesus by giving up the sin of his heart. Consequently, on the outside it appeared Dan was doing OK. Going to a counselor, still singing in the choir, answering all of Pastor's and the counselor's questions with the "correct" responses. Only Lori knew if there had really been a change. What do you do when everyone thinks everything is going fine and *you* know you are living with a man who is living a lie? And you can't prove it?

Two pastors, three counselors, two male accountability relationships, two male accountability groups, and approximately three years later they were still at square one with Dan and the marriage. What it boiled down to was Dan was not ready to face his sin and surrender completely to God and no one could force him to. No one can force another person to repentance. Conviction is God's job.

But Lori and I had been learning and growing and had come to some conclusions about Lori, her role and her choices. During these initial several years of struggle and frustration Lori began to pray for God to show her what He wanted of her. To put into practice *Psalms 139:23-24, "Search ME oh God, and know my heart; test me and know my anxious thoughts. See if there is any offensive way in ME and lead me in the way everlasting". NIV*

WHAT?

Lori needed to change? You can't be serious! After what she's been through? She is obviously innocent in all this. Right?

My husband likes to make the observation that according to God's Word *no one* is an innocent person. "There is none righteous, no not one." We all are born in sin.

Ok, ok! So what does that mean for someone in Lori's situation?

First, Lori found that she needed to get her eyes off of Dan and on to God and what He wanted to do in her life. It is hard, when we find ourselves in difficult situations not of our own making, to understand what God really wants of us. So, on a daily basis we would pray for God to show Lori what she needed to do, or change, or not do. It became very interesting when He began to show Lori some patterns in her own life that may have been hindering God's work in Dan's.

In my vast experience and studies, (you *are* laughing now aren't you?)…Ok, in my own life, I've noticed that as a woman I have my own ideas of how best to be my husband's helpmate. And *of course* I let him know exactly what I think. On a regular basis. Constantly. Because apparently he didn't hear me the first time and I can see things SO clearly. Is any of this sounding familiar or am I the only one with this problem? Well Lori had the same problem.

Lori and I could see things so clearly where Dan was concerned. We would listen to the sermons and watch Dan out of the corner of our eyes. Then, ask each other "how can he sit and listen to that and not SEE it?".

Time for a reality check. It was *God's* business how and when He is working on Dan. *"Now we see through a glass darkly"*. Boy was this a hard concept to learn. We women seem to have difficulty letting go of the reins, giving up control. It began to be a catch phrase for us. "It's a control issue".

Well, apparently it's ALWAYS a control issue. In our marriage roles, *and* with God. We would save ourselves *so* much grief if we would just let God handle our spouses and quit trying to do it for God. We began to get a clear picture that, even though she was not intending to, Lori was standing between Dan and God and in essence being a stumbling block that Dan was tripping over. Each time God would put Dan in a situation to deal with him, Lori would jump in there and tell God, "Wait a minute, I think I can handle this!". And of course, every time, she would get dumped on. Dan's focus would then be on **her** instead of where God wanted it. The more she tried to "fix it" for Dan the more he would use her as an excuse. It was never good enough. She never tried hard enough. If she would only love him like she was supposed to then he would be able to be a godly man. And on it went. She was getting beat up emotionally and in this area this *was* her own fault.

It was very difficult to get it through Lori's head that Dan's repentance or lack of it was NOT her responsibility. She could not coerce it, or manipulate it, or talk him into it, or talk to him rationally about it. She was only getting more and more frustrated as he would retreat into a shell of disinterest and passive aggressive manipulation. She couldn't even get him to make simple decisions like, should they go out to dinner or did he want dinner at all? He was in his own fantasy world and she was making all the decisions. He had abdicated his God given leadership role and she had assumed it. After all *somebody* had to do it, right? And *somebody* had to tell him what to do, right?

It was then that God directed us to the scripture verses in 1st Peter 3. Or, should I say, slapped us in the face with it. What a revelation. Such a simple passage and, actually, at first glance, rather irritating. Our focus was directed to the first four verses:

"Wives in the same way be submissive to your husbands so that, if any of them do not believe the word, they may be won over without words by the behavior of their wives. When they see the purity and reverence of your lives. Your beauty should not come from outward adornment, such as braided hair and the wearing of gold jewelry and fine clothes. Instead, it should be that gentle and quiet spirit, which is of great worth in God's sight." NIV

Our initial reaction, based on what we've been taught in this society, is to curl up our lips and be repulsed by the images these verses conjure up. Well, mine was and I can't be the only one out there who cringes when first confronted with them. After God pointedly directed me to these verses and after reading them it boiled down to two simple words I felt I had to share with Lori that would later become our simple creed to each other as women: "SHUT UP!"

"…if any of them (husbands) do not believe the word, they may be won over WITHOUT WORDS by the behavior of their wives." 1st Peter 3:1b NIV

You have GOT to be kidding, right? God definitely is not. It is the simplest of phrases but I find it is the hardest for women to actually do.

Ok, we needed to regroup, re-boot, re-evaluate. Back to the bottom line again. Is God who He says he is and can the Bible be trusted?

Anyone who tells you that being a Christian is easy is lying or is floating down the river of "denial". And anyone who tells you life *without* Christ is easier is a *bigger* liar. BUT having a personal relationship with Jesus Christ is the only way to have peace in a situation like this and to have a **sure** hope that He CAN heal and do miracles. The secular world cannot give you this hope. They would tell Lori and Dan that he was born that way and the only solution would be for Lori to divorce Dan and look for a heterosexual man and for Dan to come out of the closet, give up his traditional family and follow his "natural" gender orientation. Just think of what would have happened to this family had Lori done this. It makes my toes curl every time I think of what might have been if we had given up on not only Dan, but on God and His power.

Did Lori get angry? YES! Did she need to vent? ABSOLUTELY! Was she supposed to pretend that everything was great and put up a front at church and in front of friends and relatives? ABSOLUTELY NOT! There is a line, a benchmark, as Christians that we have to reach for in our lives. Lori had to figure out how to be real and honest and yet not dishonor Dan. Talk about a tall order. Did she fail? Sure, she did. But always, with accountability and prayer and support from other believers who knew God was in control, she would re-focus and trod on, step by step, day by day.

She would, if asked, say "yes we are having problems" *without* disclosing the sensitive nature of the situation and would ask for prayer for herself as well as Dan. They were put on the "family needs" prayer list, which, by the way, ticked Dan off. You see, *he* was the one pretending but she, with quiet dignity, would share discretely when God presented an opportunity. And our pastors did know the details, were supportive and prayed fervently for them both.

There is also a misconception, I believe, regarding the verses dealing with submission. Nowhere in scripture do I find verses that say submission is to excuse or cover up another's sin. It was not her job to convict him, that was the Holy Spirits job. But neither was she to cover up or enable his sin. Submission does not mean that if your husband asks you to be a party to his sin that in obedience or submission you participate. But it does mean with honor and respect for his position as head of your home that you decline gracefully and leave the responsibility for those choices in his lap.

Lori's counselor put it to her this way; Dan has made a plate full of poisoned food. It smells and tastes awful and it will make him sick and eventually kill him if he eats it but he wants *you* to eat it. He keeps putting it in front of you and telling you "Here, *you* eat this". Her counselor told her she needed to put the plate back in front of Dan and tell him "no, thanks, that's your food. You made it, you eat it". Again, that "shut up and let him take responsibility for his own life" concept. The hard one. The one that just about kills a woman to do but will save her life if she'll just SHUT UP! It *is* Biblical you know.

Gradually, Lori had begun to take action. She was praying. Reading the Word. Seeing a sound Biblical counselor and in an accountability relationship to keep her on track and focused daily. She had taken steps and set boundaries to protect her children from being exposed to his sin. And was learning to walk the walk of faith in a dark tunnel without seeing any light ahead, just trusting the Father of Light to direct and protect her, and for grace to "shut up". Day in, day out. She had good days and lots of bad ones but we trudged on together.

Then, one day, I received another phone call…

CHAPTER THREE

Maggie

It was spring, approximately three years into my accountability relationship with Lori. I picked up the phone as it rang and was pleasantly surprised to hear my sister-in-law's voice. Maggie and I had become friends over the nine years she and my husband's brother, Steven, had been married. We weren't really very close but we had a lot in common marrying into the same family and had shared some similar struggles as daughters-in-law. They had moved from near us, back to her hometown out of state a few years before and we spoke occasionally on the phone and always enjoyed chatting. We had not had opportunity to spend a lot of time together when they lived near but we seemed to click as friends.

But I was unprepared for what Maggie had called to tell me. She was obviously upset as she told me without preamble, that Steven was involved with another woman. She had found him at this woman's house a few nights before in the middle of the night when he hadn't come home. Again, the world tilted and things seemed to be falling apart. And again, both of them were professing born again believers, Christians. How could this be happening?

Steven is a very talented, charming man with a degree in music and a talent for writing music, directing, and playing various instruments. He had ended up as music and choir director at a Baptist church in a small farming community where he and

21

Maggie lived, just outside of a large metropolitan city. It was a little church with a handful of families who were thrilled to have someone with his obvious talent and charisma to help with their music ministry. He was the star.

Steven and Maggie's marriage had not been smooth sailing even from the beginning. Maggie had only been a baby Christian of about a year when they married and he was a Baptist minister's son. Both with very strong personalities and a bent toward selfishness, they had not practiced Biblical principles in their marriage, and in-law problems early on had driven a wedge between them. Maggie, as a new believer and having come from a non-Christian home of hard working farmers, tried to deal with things the only way she knew how. She could handle it and no *man* was going to make her submit. She was tough and capable and did not have a clue as to what the Bible said regarding the role of a wife.

Steven, on the other hand, came from a very authoritarian Christian background and believed that it was a Biblical principle that women were to submit regardless, no questions asked. And of course he *and* his father, both, were quick to inform her of her "duty". Do you see any difficulties with this situation yet? He also didn't seem to have an understanding of what *his* role as "servant leader" was. So…

She rebelled. Surprised? I didn't think so.

And he became harsh and unloving. Makes sense doesn't it? Sin is a vicious cycle that feeds on itself.

Not having a close relationship with her and most times talking superficially, I had no idea how bad things had gotten over the years. She would occasionally mention her frustration with him and his "irritating habits" but then would say "I guess it's not as bad as so and so, so and so does this and I couldn't deal with that". Always minimizing what was going on and ignoring the warning signs. Looking back there had been definite red flags.

My heart sank listening to Maggie tell me where they had ended up.

He was involved with a woman at the church. One who was going through marital problems herself.

He was denying that he was doing anything wrong. He claimed he wasn't having an affair and that nothing was going on. That Maggie didn't know anything and that she was crazy.

She had come to resent church. Making up excuses not to go. He used any excuse possible to be there. Even when there weren't services. He had to practice music. All the time. Several evenings a week and all day Sunday he would be gone. Everyone at church loved him. He was so talented and committed to them.

Maggie would be both relieved that he was out of the house, since they would only fight and get on each other's nerves, yet resent the fact that he was gone again. And as far as their intimate relationship, it was non-existent. He was sleeping on the couch.

She had suspected something for some time and when he hadn't come home that night, she tracked him down and found out he was at *her* house. She had sensed something about his relationship to this woman for some time and then when things came to a head her worst fears were confirmed.

Maggie's father owned a large farming operation where Steven worked days and had a very flexible schedule while Maggie worked full time in the city. He had been coming home during the day and spending quite a bit of time on the phone with this woman. Then they began meeting secretly.

He eventually admitted to seeing this woman but continued to insist that he was doing nothing wrong. After all, he hadn't "slept" with her so he had not had an affair although he did admit to some physical involvement. They lived in the country, isolated to a certain extent and Maggie had no one close, especially at the church that she could go to. She had no Christian friends close enough to call and being a small church and community, gossip spread like wild fire. Those in the church who found out were simply shaking their heads. "You poor thing", and "He's in love with her, honey", as if there was nothing to do now. Things were going from bad to worse and out of desperation not knowing where to turn, Maggie picked up the phone and called me.

Now what? What do I tell Maggie? Knowing Steven as well as I did and his history with relationships, it didn't look good. And apparently this wasn't about sex; he was *in love* with this woman. How do you compete with that? Steven, having kept himself emotionally distant from his own wife for almost 10 years was feeling things he hadn't in a long time. He wanted to leave. He wanted to be with this woman. But he had been raised being taught that divorce wasn't an option and was struggling between what he was feeling and what he had been taught. At this point he was looking for a loophole in scripture to get him out of his marriage.

As I listened to Maggie I was praying. 'So, Lord, here we go again. And for that matter, why me?'

'Obedience' was the quiet response. 'But Lord, I'm not a counselor. I don't have a degree, I'm not qualified to deal with this.'

But God didn't want me to give my opinion, or to tell these women what to do. He simply wanted me to use the spiritual gifts *He* had given me and point them to Scripture and *His* answers. He would use the foolish to confound the wise of the world. He even wanted to use *me*. The seriousness of these situations and the responsibility of the position I had been put in was humbling and very frightening. As I would walk these paths with these women, I would learn more about who God is than I ever had before and God would allow me the privilege to be there when He performed miracles that even fellow believers said couldn't happen.

Only by God's grace and power would we get through this struggle together.

"So Lord, what do I say?"

And God said "Tell her to SHUT UP." 1st Peter 3...

CHAPTER 4

"1st Peter WHO?"

What do you mean, SHUT UP? Are you kidding? Not again, Lord. Not this time. Doesn't she need to tell him what he's doing? He obviously can't see what he's doing to their family. He doesn't know how much this is hurting Maggie. Or what it's going to do to his children. And besides, it's just plain wrong. Sinful. Someone needs to TELL him that. And who better than his wife who is feeling it and can see it clearly. The injured party. The victim. Right?

WRONG!

Maggie and I read 1st Peter 3:1-4 together and tried to decide what that meant for her in this situation. Completely shut up? How in the world could she do that and live in the same house with a man who openly admitted he didn't love her anymore?

Time to step back and get the big picture. It was time for Maggie to get her eyes off of her husband and onto God. How was that going to help her? It didn't change the situation. No, but when we get our eyes off of our circumstances and other people and on Him, things start to happen. And it's usually in US not our circumstances that begin to change. Maggie had to learn what God wanted to teach her regardless of Steven's actions or reaction. The more we focus on the other person, the more hopeless things become. The more we focus on God the more hope we have and our faith is strengthened.

The God who is able to do more than we can even ask or think was asking her to get out of the way so He could work on Steven and at the same time trust Him with what He was teaching her about being a Godly wife. That's a tall order for any woman. What a totally ridiculous thing to expect. After all, she is only human. How much is she supposed to put up with and let him get away with?

Ok, so is God who He says He is or not? WELL? If the answer is yes then why would we choose to do anything less than what He asks? 1st Peter WHO? Says WHAT? Ok God, it's time to take you at your Word. This is where the rubber meets the road.

By this time I was spending time daily with *both* Lori and Maggie. Still talking on the phone, Maggie out of state and Lori across town. I remember feeling literally consumed by prayer. To "pray without ceasing" became a tangible reality for me more than it had ever been in my life. Both Lori and Maggie were also experiencing a prayer closet like never before. Neither of them had met or spoken with each other at this point but I had asked permission of each of them to share the other's story and they agreed. Somehow knowing that someone else was walking the same path at the same time was an encouragement. They both had to apply 1st Peter 3 to their lives and ask God what that meant for them each on a daily basis.

For Lori it meant not initiating *anything* with Dan. Nothing. She had been doing his job *and* trying to do hers and then nagging him about why he couldn't see the mess he was in. She needed to fulfill her "role" but distance herself from the relationship. God began to show her patterns in her own life where she enable those she loved and took responsibility for their actions thinking that was her job. She had to struggle with giving up false guilt and recognize that true love was, at times, tough love.

I remember Lori asking me, "Aren't we supposed to have an intimate relationship in a godly marriage? Am I not supposed to share with Dan how I feel or what my needs are?"

My answer was "Are you married to a godly man right now?"

Her answer, "No, obviously not."

"And how do you feel when you've shared your feelings with him and tried to communicate?"

The answer was *always*, "Frustrated and hurt".

Exactly!

You see these men were not walking with God and had chosen sin. What makes us think as wives if our husbands are rebelling against God that they will just sit down and listen to *us* and say "Oh, I see what you're saying, you're right. I'll just kneel right here and pray and take care of that."

WAKE UP LADIES! I don't know *anyone*, male *or* female, that it's that easy for when we are in open rebellion against God, do you? If he doesn't want to hear from God what makes you think he wants to hear it from you? It just perpetuates the sin cycle. So save yourself the frustration and put it in God's hands. Shut up and get out of the way. It always turns out best when we trust God even if we can't see the light at the end of the tunnel. Remember that God built the tunnel and He knows best when to turn that light on, the switch is in His hands.

It also may require giving up what *we* think the ideal marriage relationship is and wait for God to give us *His* plan for our marriage.

There is a story about a little girl who went to the dime store one day with her mother. The little girl spotted some play jewelry and begged her mommy for a string of plastic pearls. Her mother bought the pearls for her and she put them on beaming with pride. She loved those plastic pearls. They were beautiful. She wore them day and night. To school and at play and after awhile they began to look a little rough and tattered. The paint had begun to peel off the beads and the string was dirty. But she didn't see that. She just loved those pearls. Each night before bed she would climb up onto her daddy's lap and snuggle in front of the fireplace. She felt very loved and secure in his arms.

One night, while sitting in his lap before bed her daddy asked her, "Honey, do you love me?"

"Oh yes, daddy. I love you very much."

He held out his hand and gently asked, "will you give me your pearls?"

"Oh no, daddy. I can't take them off. I love my pearls." He quietly hugged her and she got down and went off to bed.

The next evening she climbed up in his lap again to snuggle and again he asked, "Honey, do you love me?"

"You know I love you daddy. You're the best daddy ever."

"Will you give me your pearls?" He asked again.

She slowly shook her head; "I don't want to, daddy. They're the only ones I have." Again she got down and went off to bed.

29

The next evening it was time for bed and the little girl was quiet as she climbed up into her daddy's lap. She knew what he was going to ask.

"Honey, do you love me?"

With downcast eyes she simply nodded yes.

"Will you give me your pearls?"

She didn't answer but slowly reached up to take them off as a tear slipped down her face.

Her daddy took her prized possession, those dirty, ragged pearls, and threw them into the fire. But then as she clung to him sobbing, he reached into his pocket and pulled out a beautiful string of real pearls and placed them around her neck.

Now which pearls would you rather have?

It is the process of giving up that is the most difficult for each of us but God wants to give us the real thing. God's pearls are authentic and eternal and when He gives them to us we kick ourselves for not giving up sooner.

And then for Maggie, as she and I worked through this together, it became quite comical.

9:00am the phone rings. It's Maggie. Without preamble, "So tell my why I'm doing this again?".

"Did Jesus hang on the cross and die for you?" I shoot back.

"OK, ok. But this sure isn't fun."

"As I recall the Bible didn't promise you fun."

Another call, "So, how long am I supposed to live with a man who hates me and loves another woman?"

Again, "Did Jesus die on a cross for you?"

"ALRIGHT, alright. I got the picture."

How long? However long it would take God to do a work in *Maggie*, not necessarily Steven. I believe we have to agree with God because of who *He* is, not for what He may or may not do for us now. "Though He slay me, yet I will serve Him." God has already paid the penalty for my sin and I will serve him even if I am thrown into the fiery furnace or killed. God wants to teach us maturity not manipulation. He is not the big "sugar daddy" in the sky to give us whatever we want just because we are uncomfortable or in pain. He gives us His best, even if it hurts at first. If Steven never told Maggie he loved her again, what would be her response to God's command for her to be a godly wife?

Well, during our conversations, which were several a day, she would share her feelings and vent, which is normal and healthy. But the response had to always be "Get your eyes off Steven and on God". What are *you* to do today? Not Steven. You can vent but don't wallow in it.

1st Peter 3 became a daily discipline. We tried to come up with word pictures to help us both focus on what that meant. Maggie said that to her it was like being a dog meeting its owner at the door. No words, no expectations, just quietly licking it's owners hand. I know some of you are having a problem with this one but, hey, it got us through. Radio broadcasts such as Family Life Today with Dennis Rainey and Focus on the Family with James Dobson have had many programs dealing with the role of women and wives talking about similar attitudes, so we listened and learned and tried to just have fun with it. We would laugh and say "Be a dog, girlfriend".

EXCUSE ME? As in the "role", not as a degrading personal description. Some of the other girls later on would come up with "get in a FOG", as in Focus On God. You see, when we are there to encourage one another, even in the seemingly small things like a word or a phrase, it lightens the burden. And a sense of humor goes along way in helping to make the joy of the Lord a reality at times like this. Hand him his coffee and *walk away.* Serve him dinner and *walk away.* And of course you *need* a sense of humor to be able do this and not feel like you're losing your mind. Many people thought these girls had already gone over the edge just to stay in these situations.

At this point there was little need for much of any type of conversation past the basic "we need milk" or "can you to pick up the kids". Steven was hostile and harsh and she needed to emotionally distance herself from him yet still follow through on her role as Godly wife, which, by the way, was a new concept for Maggie so it actually kept her busy and focused much of the time. She had good days and many bad ones, but God was beginning to get her attention much in the same way He had begun to get Lori's.

Maggie also realized that she could not blame the other woman either. Not that this woman wasn't responsible before God for her actions, but Steven had made his own choices and so had Maggie and she realized she had not been there for her husband and someone else had. She began to pray for both of them and when you begin to pray in earnest for your "enemies", God tends to take away the bitterness and give you a heart of forgiveness. Now don't get me wrong, there was still anger and hurt in the situation. Some times when we were being silly we would talk about doing ridiculous things like taking lawn fertilizer and spreading it in the shape of an "A" on her yard so when the grass came up it would be obvious. We never would *do* anything like that but, being human, sometimes it would alleviate some of the tension to joke around and laugh. It sounds irreverent but it was never malicious and many times helped let off steam.

In the mean time, everyone in the small church had heard various versions of "the situation". The Pastor and one of the elders attempted to reach out to Steven but their attempts were rejected and it became very uncomfortable for everyone concerned. Unfortunately, the leaders and church body did not pursue the issue and inadvertently added to the gossip by not dealing with the situation. There was no discipline or accountability. Maggie felt as if she had no support as they seemed to turn their backs, not only on her but Steven also.

Steven began avoiding church leaders, and eventually began to give up his responsibilities, while still maintaining a relationship with this woman. No one wanted to deal with the elephant in the room and was ignoring the sin eating away at the church from the inside out.

Maggie had begun to draw clear boundaries in the relationship while trying to find the balance of silence, and knowing when to shut up. Boundaries are important. They help define our roles. Godly boundaries would protect Maggie and help her to follow through on her responsibilities as well as make it clear that Steven was responsible for his own choices and actions. This is *not* about being a doormat. Being a Godly wife involves a proactive attitude toward my role. It is *not* a passive, martyrdom that God has called us to. I believe this involves setting boundaries that help a woman stay within the responsibilities of her God given role. As a woman recognizes this she is able to get out of the way and let the Holy Spirit work on her husband. It's the 1st Peter 3 thing again.

Not being one to pretend, Maggie challenged Steven to call his parents and tell them that they were having problems. She gave him the choice, if he wouldn't she would. She felt that they needed all the prayer and moral support they could get. He did end up calling them and sharing a slightly distorted version of what was going on but at least they knew and hopefully would add Godly advise or at least prayer support.

It became apparent that things were happening with Steven. During the first few months after the situation had come to a head, Maggie worked on what it meant to "be a dog" and as she began to get out of the way with God showing her the areas she needed to change, interesting things began to happen.

I find human behavior, and the paths we allow sin to take us down in our lives, fascinating. In all the situations I have observed with women coping with husbands in rebellion to God, it has never failed that they seem to follow the same patterns, as we all do. Human nature is human nature. Sin is sin. And the Bible clearly spells out the consequences of unrepentant sin. "Be sure your sin will find you out". Regardless of the situation, background, or specific sin, the response seems to be the same. When God has exposed the sin the initial reaction is denial, deceit, and blame shifting. "You don't know what you're talking about, there's nothing going on." "I haven't done anything wrong." "You don't even know me, you don't care." And on and on.

Then comes the irrational anger and accusations. We want to push emotional buttons. If I can get you to react in anger and sin then that justifies my sin. "See how you are? That's why this will never work." "You've never supported me." "You've never been a good wife (or husband)." The words *always* and *never* tend to come up often. Many times it deteriorates to name calling or derogatory statements about family members just to get a negative response. We know best where our spouses are vulnerable and it's like cornering a wounded animal, we get vicious in our self-preservation. Anything to take the blame and focus off of our sin and us.

Then panic and paranoia, when we feel we are losing control and cannot manipulate the situation. It's a scary thing to be faced with who we are in light of God's holiness. We forget about His love and forgiveness and continue to try and "fix" it without actually submitting to His authority in our lives. We begin to try and make deals with God and to placate those around us. Jumping through hoops that we think will alleviate the guilt and condemnation, telling ourselves that it's external.

"It's *them,* they don't understand. If I can just get them all off my back this will go away."

Or "It's my circumstances." Or "I come from a dysfunctional family, it's their fault."

Once again, we need to get God's big picture in order to be able to get through these times. How can a woman "1st Peter 3 it", as we liked to call it, in the middle of all this chaos. When we are distracted by the specific battles we are in we forget that God has won the war. In order to survive we need to trust our Commander implicitly and follow Him and His orders in the midst of the battle. And not just to survive but to ultimately live victorious, abundant, God-honoring lives. As our pastor likes to say, "We are not 'copers', we are conquerors." He has promised us this in His Word if we will only obey.

So what are God's commands in situations like these women were facing? First we needed to agree that God IS who He says He is and His Word is Truth. So in light of that, if we want to truly be obedient to God we *must* obey his Word even if it doesn't seem to make sense, especially in the secular world.

But be prepared. Following the Commander means taking the off beaten paths through the jungle of testing and the battles of growth and testing our faith and resolve to the very core of our being. It means, if we truly surrender our will to the Great Commander, He will take us through battles that will expose the deepest, darkest, fears we have and make us face them.

Psalms 139:23,24 "Search me, O God, and know my heart; test me and know my anxious thoughts. See if there be any offensive way in me, and lead me in the way everlasting." NIV

So, hang on, here we go. Are you ready girls?

CHAPTER 5

"Who ME?"

As I said before, human nature is human nature and sin is sin and Dan and Steven both went through the same stages. Different personalities and backgrounds, and seemingly, different specific sins, but the same results. Each went through these different phases to one extent or another, avoiding responsibility for their choices.

Maggie had gotten referrals for counseling on her own and had found a biblically sound Christian counseling center and Steven had agreed to go. They both liked their counselor. He had a very direct style, at times confrontational. Both of them would say what was expected and then would go through the motions of carrying out any assignment the counselor would ask of them. But often, the hour-long drive to and from the sessions was filled with awkward silence or uncomfortable anger.

During these first few months things had settled into a sort of mundane pattern. Maggie would, daily, struggle to shut up and follow through in her role as wife and Steven remained distant and uncommunicative. There were times when Maggie had overwhelming feelings that Steven was still seeing this other woman. She would call home in the middle of the day and the line would be busy or he would dress up and leave the house without any explanation. At these times when she just *knew,* she would confront Steven. Not ask or argue but she would simply say, "I know you've seen or talked to her, just so you know", and she would tell him that he was going to, at some point, have to make a choice. Usually, one way or another her "feeling" would be confirmed. It was as if the Holy Spirit was letting her know when something was happening. She didn't need to know the details, or pull them out of Steven. She just needed to let Steven know that he wasn't getting away with anything. You see, God knows the thoughts and intents of our heart but when we are in rebellion we think we are fooling everyone, including God. She was drawing boundaries and learning about tough love. She had told Steven that she was willing to work on the marriage and that she knew God could heal their relationship, but that if he wanted to leave, it was his choice but *he* was going to have to make it. No one can force another to do anything against his or her will. Besides, who really would want someone to stay just because they felt "forced" and not because they chose to or wanted to?

At times when it would get confrontational, it would get ugly. Steven would say terrible things to push her buttons and get her to react. If he could get her to sin, as I said before, it would justify his. So the cycle for Steven continued. Denial, deceit, blame shifting, paranoia, irrational anger, manipulation and appeasement. And on it went.

And the phone calls from Maggie. "How long am I supposed to live like this?" And "Tell me why I'm doing this again?"

It seemed as if nothing was happening. Day in and day out. Stress, frustration, and pain. There were days when Maggie could hardly concentrate at work with the crippling emotional pain she was feeling and the knowledge that Steven could, at that moment, be meeting with another woman.

All the while we would be praying on a daily, moment by moment, basis for her and Steven and even the other woman. We would need to refocus daily. Getting our eyes off of Steven and the situation and back on Jesus and what He wanted for Maggie. She still had to take responsibility for her part in the mess they found themselves in.

"WHAT? ME APPOLOGIZE?"

"Have you been a godly wife all these years?"

"Well…no... But..."

"NO BUTS. If you've done wrong then you need to take care of it, right?"

"But apologize to HIM? ME? You've got to be kidding. Look what *he's* done."

"And what did Jesus do for you?"

"OK. Ok."

"We'll pray about it. You can do this, with God's help."

Well, Maggie had admitted that she had not been a godly wife for the past 10 years but she hadn't done anything to take care of it. She knew she had not honored her husband nor had she been submissive. Now she was ready to take responsibility for her sin. She would need to apologize to the very husband who said he hated her and was in love with another woman. That was difficult enough, but God wasn't through with her yet.

Another afternoon and another phone call from Maggie. This time she was sobbing. Even in an emotional situation Maggie is not an emotional woman. She is not weepy by any sense of the word but this day she was literally sobbing. I thought for sure that Steven had moved out. But no, this wasn't about Steven. God was dealing with Maggie.

"I'm mortified." She choked out.

"My most horrible, embarrassing secret is being told around town."

I couldn't imagine. Then she brokenly began to tell me what she had carefully kept hidden for years. She had a temper. Well, don't we all? But, no, I didn't understand. She had a problem with abuse. Spousal abuse. She would get angry and "go off" on Steven. She would lose control and beat on him, throw things, even go after him with a hoe or rake, screaming and yelling. He had only gotten physical in return in the recent past months during this whole mess. He'd had enough apparently, and he had shared this secret outside their marriage, with the other woman no less, and now it was fodder for the local gossips at the beauty salon in town.

Maggie also confessed to an Internet relationship with someone. In her rebellious anger she had gotten involved in a chat room talking with a man on the Internet. He made her feel attractive and wanted but when the man asked to meet her she had gotten scared and terminated the relationship. Steven had discovered her on the computer with this man during a chat session. It wasn't long after that that Maggie had found out about Steven and the other woman.

Humiliation, embarrassment, and shame. Maggie was definitely broken and she had no one to blame but herself. God had peeled back the layers and exposed a sin that had festered into a cancerous tumor in Maggie's life. It was time to confess and repent.

Now, what?

It was getting more and more complicated. How can we go on from here? He hates her and is in love with another woman. They had both spent years verbally and emotionally abusing one another. And she had physically abused and emotionally emasculated Steven with her temper.

This seems impossible doesn't it? Just like Dan and Lori. No hope. It's all too far-gone.

This was a turning point for both Maggie and Lori in their growth. The "Who Me?" question became, "it's ME Lord" and from where I sat this is where things began to really get exciting.

CHAPTER SIX

"It's ME Lord."

Confessing and repenting is a bitter pill to swallow but, oh, what cleansing medicine. The great physician began to truly cleanse and heal Maggie from that point on. She had begun the change as she daily gave over her will to the Heavenly Father, but now he had stripped away the sin and infection that had been poisoning her life. She began to have a passion for God and His will for her life. It wasn't just going through steps to save her marriage, it was *living* for the God who saved her and gave His life for her. You see, we cannot "change" to manipulate our circumstances or people. That is not genuine repentance. What we do, we have to do out of obedience to Jesus Christ and for Him alone because He first loved us and died for us. Maggie and Lori had to do what God expected of them regardless of what their husbands decided to do. Even if they left them.

It began to make a noticeable difference in Maggie. Even Steven noticed. But instead of seeing positive change he accused her of trying to manipulate him. In his own sin he refused to see what God was doing in the life of his wife. He had no trust for her, but of course, she had destroyed that with her anger over the years.

Should she keep doing what God wanted her to? Even in the face of her husband's ridicule? Absolutely! She wasn't doing it because her husband deserved it or for him at all. God had commanded her to submit and honor her husband *as unto the Lord.* Whether Steven appreciated it and believed her or not. Further on in 1st Peter chapter 3 it even talks about suffering for doing right.

Maggie had apologized but Steven hadn't really heard her. But before God, Maggie had done the right thing and God began to bless her walk with Him. She began to get to know the Savior in a very personal and intimate way that she had never experienced before. God became her portion, her all in all. When we *"turn our eyes upon Jesus and look full in His wonderful face, the things of earth grow strangely dim in the light of His glory and grace."*

We considered Job who, unlike Maggie and even Lori, had not contributed to his terrible circumstances yet when everything was taken from him said *"the Lord giveth and the Lord taketh away, blessed be the name of the Lord" Job 1:21 KJV.* Talk about trust and faith. This was what God was trying to teach us. It wasn't about Steven or Dan. It wasn't about marriage or personal happiness. It wasn't about adultery or pornography or homosexuality. It was about our awesome God and who He is. Do we really believe Him and want the kind of relationship with Him that He wants with us? Do we want to risk missing out on the only relationship that is truly eternal with the only One who will *never* fail or reject us, for momentary comfort and fleeting happiness?

To most it seems this attitude is lunacy. Even fellow believers who were aware of the situations would have the attitude that Job's wife and friends did "curse God and die", there is no hope, why continue to suffer?

God's Word would say to them and us, *"I consider that our present sufferings are not worth comparing with the glory that will be revealed in us." Romans 8:18* NIV

Are we as Christians today even reading the Bible? And if we are, do we actually believe it? Because as near as I can tell we sure aren't living like we do. It was very discouraging for these women to hear the negative comments and focus of other believers who seemed to only see the human circumstances and the impossibility of the situations. Did they even know who God is?

Lori and Maggie began to see the need to distance themselves from those who would pull their attention away from Jesus. This meant emotional distance even from their husbands. Oh they still had to work daily at being godly wives but they began to focus on God in earnest. God began to use the "it's me, Lord" attitude in their lives to cultivate rich ground for growth and fruit in their lives.

Lori was recognizing her patterns of enabling and rescuing and had begun to set firm boundaries and follow through. When Dan would bait her by asking vague questions expecting her to come up with the meaning and then go ahead and do all the talking, she would simply just look at him waiting for him to be more specific. It would anger and frustrate him that he could not get her to "eat the food he had placed in front of her". He would continue to try and manipulate Lori to get her to take responsibility for his actions or lack of them. It would take time for her to figure out the specific boundaries that she needed to set and how to respond. Lori also had to deal with feelings of false guilt. That somehow in all this and even in her previous marriage she was still to blame for others mistakes. She did indeed have to take responsibility for her own sin before God but Lori had also spent years feeling guilty for things she had no control over. This was a huge issue for her and part of why she was always trying to "fix things" for everyone. If only she were good enough then maybe these things wouldn't happen or people wouldn't do the things they were doing that hurt.

Lori learned that the only person she could fix was herself with the help of the Holy Spirit. This was actually a very freeing concept for Lori to realize. You see, to submit ourselves to God is a positive, proactive process, not the negative, passive one that most of us think. When we are focused on God and what He wants us to do then we don't have time to worry about what others are or aren't doing. It's just God and us. It made it so much easier for Lori to let go of that guilt and get out of the way. Big things were happening with Lori but it seemed Dan still was going nowhere.

Maggie, on the other hand, needed to recognize the patterns of anger and abuse in her life. It is interesting that once God brought her face to face with her sin and she was broken before Him, the bondage was also broken. She still needed to take a cold hard look at her life and make changes but it was no longer impossible. Maggie began looking at verses dealing with anger and found biblical based articles on controlling anger from various sources. She was stunned to realize that she didn't have to lose control, that even the act of losing control was her choice. We would talk about the things that happened before she would "go off" and began to see how she and Steven would verbally push each other's emotional buttons. Again, it was about getting the big picture and recognizing what was happening. Once she realized this she found it much easier to "not go there" with Steven. This began to change the dynamics of their relationship also. She was getting out of the way so God could deal with her husband, but regardless of what Steven decided to do, she was working on what God expected of her.

Both Maggie and Lori were changing, becoming 1st Peter 3 wives. And as they grew their whole demeanor changed. The quiet and gentle spirit was showing through. Now, I believe that when the Bible speaks of a quiet and gentle spirit it is not necessarily referring to personality. I believe it is an inner peace and quiet confidence that shines through no matter the circumstances. A calm assurance that comes from knowing Who is in control and Who we are serving. A noticeable maturity regardless of your personality type. With it comes the realization that I don't have to take control, and I cannot change my husband, but I serve the God who can do anything and knows more about what is going on with my husband than I do. I can leave it in His almighty hands.

This is what was happening to Maggie and Lori. The ability to not panic or bolt or freak out when things appeared to be out of control. The quality that comes from God that allowed Maggie to stand, unemotional in the face of terrible, hurtful, verbal attacks. That allowed Lori to stand silent and firm when she was faced daily with criticism and passive manipulation and both having no intimacy whatsoever with their husbands.

It had now been four years for Lori and months for Maggie. How long did God expect them to stay in these situations? They had recognized their sin and made changes. Surely God would relieve their emotional suffering now. He wouldn't expect them to continue on in these relationships when it was apparent that their husbands were not going to change, right?

Excuse me. **DID JESUS DIE ON THE CROSS FOR YOU?** Yes! Well, then, however long it takes to accomplish His will is however long it takes. PERIOD!

At this point Maggie and Lori still had not met or communicated with each other directly. But they continued to be aware of each other's situations. We would eventually find a way to connect to each other and communicate together but it would still be some time before this would take place. But we had time. Will it be worth it? Guess you'll have to read on and see. After all, we had only just begun...

CHAPTER SEVEN

What ifin'

There is one thing that I have found that Maggie, Lori, myself, and any woman I have spent time talking to, tends to struggle with. It is what I like to call "what ifin'". It's the response we have to anything that we are asked to do that, in our perception, threatens our security.

"But what if..."

"If I do this, what if he does this?"

"What if he never..."

We like to know the outcome before we risk whatever it is. What if...?

We all do it but there comes a point when it's not just 'what ifin' and it becomes unbelief and sin and a stumbling block in our growth with the Lord. We think we are questioning circumstances, covering our bases, making sure we have all the information we need to make a decision. It's how we are as women when it comes to our families and relationships. We want to protect our kids, our homes and marriages and ourselves. But in some circumstances we are actually questioning God's authority in our lives and doubting His love and sovereignty. Does he really expect me to do this? But what if...?

Lori had more of a problem with this than Maggie did. They both had to deal with the 'what ifs' but Maggie tends to like a challenge and say to God, 'ok what's the plan, let's do it' whereas Lori becomes paralyzed by fear of doing the wrong thing. But what if this doesn't work? What if he leaves? What if I say the wrong thing or draw the wrong boundary and it pushes him into the gay lifestyle? Tons of 'what ifs' for Lori. The false guilt and lack of trust was just about killing her.

The 'what ifs' will totally immobilize you if you let them. That is where study of God's Word, prayer and accountability are a must. We need to get to know Jesus so intimately that we know what our role and responsibility is and don't second-guess God. We need to leave the 'what ifs' up to God and walk by faith, not by sight.

Lori had to realize that even if she did everything perfectly Dan could still choose to leave. Once again, you cannot act or react thinking that you can control or manipulate someone else's response, they are responsible for their own choices. Yes, we can be stumbling blocks to another if we are not walking where Jesus wants us to walk, but ultimately we each have a choice to make, even if someone else is wrong, we are not excused. We each need to discover what God wants out of us individually and then leave others' decisions to them and God.

What ifin' is blatant worry over things we have no control over. God's Word tells us in Matthew 6 verses 25 through the end of the chapter not to worry or "what if". What is our focus to be?

"But seek first his kingdom and his righteousness and all these things will be given to you as well. Therefore do not worry about tomorrow, for tomorrow will worry about itself. Each day has enough trouble of its own." Matt 6:33-34 NIV

"Do not be anxious about anything, but in everything, by prayer and petition, with thanksgiving, present your requests to God and the peace of God, which transcends all understanding will guard your hearts and your minds in Christ Jesus." Phil 4:6-7 NIV

So according to God's word if it is serious enough to worry about we need to be praying and having prayed leave it in God's hands. These verses are not just for good times, good marriages, or just the small trials in life. God means for these verses to be applied in the overwhelming trials and humanly impossible circumstances in our lives. That's when they become real to us.

Is God who the Bible says he is? Or does this really work?

Satan wants nothing more than to paralyze us in our walk with God, rendering us useless to the Kingdom and cause of Christ, and in the process, rob us of the peace and joy that God gives us freely if we just believe Him and take Him at His word.

We need to face our circumstances honestly and place them before the throne of God and then leave the worry to Him. We can not afford to play mind games with ourselves and say "it's not so bad" and not deal with our situations and sin head on. Yet we cannot afford to be so overcome by circumstance that we 'what if' ourselves into a state of immobility, getting our eyes off of who God is and His power. I have often heard my pastor describe our lives as Christians as being on the straight and narrow path and that there is a ditch on either side of the road. Satan doesn't care which ditch he gets you is as long as you are not on the path God wants you on. Either way, either ditch, we become ineffective and distracted and end up missing out on where God wants to take us.

So Maggie and Lori had to deal with the "what ifin" patterns in their lives. As they did, they found it was easier to trust God's direction. But, what next? Where would God take Lori and Maggie? I would often tell them 'fasten your seat belts we're in for an exciting ride'. As the months went by this became more and more true as the Holy Spirit did a work of grace in these women but there seemed to be no apparent change in the hearts of their husbands. Trusting God became an extreme test of faith. For Maggie, fall would seem to grow even darker...

CHAPTER EIGHT

"I Quit"

As imperfect humans, there are times in our lives when we seem to run out of steam. Even as Christians we grow weary and faint and it becomes hard for us to just stand, let alone have the energy to move forward.

Maggie and Steven had spent months in counseling and then been told they didn't need to come anymore. They had all the information they needed to make this work they just needed to commit to do it and obey God's Word. But their relationship at home had not changed. For months Steven had been distant and at times polite but made no move toward Maggie in any way. Maggie continued to work on her role as a wife and emotionally distance herself from Steven to be able to 1st Peter 3 it.

But by fall things had started to deteriorate with Steven again. He had, by this time stopped going to church altogether. Their roles had reversed. Remember Maggie was the one who had not been attending church and had resented Steven's involvement. Now Maggie felt she needed all the spiritual food she could digest and made it a priority. She had even followed through in water baptism which until that summer she had argued she didn't need to do to serve the Lord. God had really broken her and she was willing to do whatever He asked.

But Steven began accusing her of going to church and talking to everyone about him. He became even more paranoid and defensive even when she had said nothing. He would say things like "You all think you know..." "You don't know me"... And on it would go.

She couldn't go to any church activity without accusations or ugly confrontations. He would be trying to push her buttons again. He was looking for an excuse. For justification for what he was choosing. It must be her fault, or the church's. Everyone was a hypocrite and we were all out to destroy him. Everyone except this woman.

After months where it had appeared he had stopped seeing this woman, he got caught again. He was seen in public with her. He fell again. This time harder. Maggie found notes and lyrics to songs he had written to her and to her parents. Was this ever going to end?

We continued to speak on the phone daily. Sometimes several times a day. She was still working full time and trying to concentrate. She was trying to protect her young children from the situation. Day in and day out. No change.

She got to a point where she couldn't stand it. She knew she couldn't control Steven and had confronted him with what she knew and basically had told him he had a choice to make. At some point he would need to either leave and go to the other woman, or stay and work on the marriage but he couldn't have both. She simply presented the choices. But the strain was getting to her. She had to get out and take a break so she packed up the kids and left for the weekend telling Steven she was going to his family. She came to our house to relax and regroup.

There are times when physical distance is necessary. She couldn't make the decision for Steven and she couldn't control what he would do if left alone.

She needed to get alone with God and gain some strength to go on. I'm not sure if anything happened with Steven that weekend but for Maggie it was needed. She went home encouraged and rested.

Steven had not changed. He continued to accuse, belittle, berate, and make irrational statements. As the Holy Spirit turned up the heat on him, he seemed to turn up the heat on Maggie.

The holidays were terrible. Christmas with the entire family was awkward. Maggie had had another 'premonition' that he had seen *her* just before they came up for family Christmas. But again he just remained distant with the family, avoiding anything but superficial conversation.

When they returned home after the holidays Steven began to get even angrier. Maggie wasn't sure what was going on or if she could continue to take it. I remember one day, around February, she called me in the morning from work.

"I'm over it. I'm done doing this. I quit. I want out." Her tone was cold and emotionless.

It scared me. I am also not easily given to tears but I began to cry. I knew this was a turning point. It could go either way for her right then and the outcome scared me to death.

"Please don't give up. Please don't give up on God. Not now."

We had spent months talking about what God wanted in our lives. Is He real? Did it matter? Can He do what the Bible says? Is the Bible truth? Did Jesus really die on the cross for Maggie? Going over it at this point didn't matter. It was down to the wire. Would she choose to believe it and act on it or wasn't it worth the pain and effort? I don't even remember what I said or what her specific response was. I just know that at some point she chose God, whatever the cost. Each time God asked Maggie to submit to His Word and trust Him, as she surrendered to His will, there would be a time of peace and growth. Each time He would give her direction and she would feel a confidence in acting on whatever He was directing her to do. The next area became dealing with the church issue.

It had been months since Steven had gone anywhere to church. He continued to accuse her of talking to everyone and spreading "gossip" each time she left the house to go. How could she remove this stumbling block? How could she get out of the way so he could not accuse her even though it wasn't true?

We talked quite a bit about the situation and she was having a hard time dealing with the conflict every time she wanted to go to church. So, I said, "why not stay home for a while?" Radical thinking? It certainly didn't make sense. But we weren't talking about forever. And certainly not about being in a position where she wouldn't be accountable or getting spiritually fed. She was not getting real biblical support from the small local body they had been attending and the other woman's family was very involved in the church and one of the long time pillars. Everyone seemed to want to ignore the situation and hope it would go away. It was the proverbial "elephant in the room no one wanted to deal with".

Maggie prayed about it and made the decision to stay home with Steven. His reaction was interesting. "Aren't you going to church?" he would ask.

"No, not if you're not." She simply let him know that when *he* was ready to go back to church, she would gladly follow him to the church of his choice. This was a 180degree change from the old Maggie. She would have never just *followed* her husband anywhere. God was changing her and Steven was noticing.

It didn't mean that the pain and hurt were all gone nor did the circumstances change immediately, but Maggie began to truly give up control in everything to God. She was recognizing that God was peeling back the layers and each layer would bring new submission, and new trust in the God who loved her enough to die for her.

It would be a year later, almost 2 years from when everything had come to a head, that the miraculous would occur.

CHAPTER NINE

He Loves Me Not! He Loves Me!

I don't know how many times during that 2-year period that Maggie repeatedly asked me "How long am I supposed to do this?" Again and again I would reply "As long as God asks you to."

The last time that she remembered Steven telling her how he really felt about her was in a conversation they had dealing with his parents and their reaction to the situation. Maggie had told Steven that she thought his mother hated her and his response was "I hated you long before my mother hated you."

So, there it was. He had said it. She had to deal with it. Not only was he in love with another woman but he *hated* Maggie. Did she really have to live in the same house with a man who openly hated her? She had lost her emotional security, humbled herself and admitted her sin to God and apologized to Steven. She had given up church and her body of believers. Her relationship with her parents was strained because they were not Christians and did not understand her decisions and reactions to the situation. She had no pride left. She had given up the right to kick him out or leave herself and she willingly made him coffee and did his laundry. Was she a doormat? ABSOLUTELY NOT! She had a plan. God's plan. How was she to continue to implement it in the face of the impossible?

At the risk of being redundant or repetitive, she needed to FOCUS ON GOD and get her eyes off of Steven. In the 2 years of our intense relationship it took saying it and repeating it thousands of times. Daily. Reading the Word *daily*. ACTING on it *daily* until it became as natural as breathing.

I kept assuring her that when God did the miraculous, her life would be different than it had ever been before. Her marriage would be better than it had ever been. Her life would be different. Actually it already was. If God only changed her and Steven continued to be in rebellion, *she* was still different and even better having submitted to God's direction and authority. God makes beauty from ashes. Don't ever think otherwise.

The problem is that most women think they just want what they had *before* it all fell apart. They would rather not know the worst and continue to live in ignorant bliss. I find that one of the most difficult things to understand. Why would anyone want a relationship less than God's best? We would rather close our eyes and pretend than change. We are afraid of the unknown so we want the "honeymoon" experience again rather than growth and intimacy. We are fools to settle for less.

I don't know about you but I wouldn't want to go back to the first few years for anything. God's plan for our marriage relationships gives us spiritual depth and intimacy that we can never know outside of His will. After over 20 years of marriage I can truly say it gets better each year. It isn't always easy, but God always honors obedience and the rewards are most definitely worth the pain. Remember, *"I consider that our present sufferings are not worth comparing with the glory that will be revealed in us." Romans 8:32 NIV*

Before this crisis, Steven would occasionally tell Maggie he loved her. Nothing really meaningful just expected. After admitting he hated her, he said nothing. He wasn't pretending anymore but it was painful for Maggie to know the truth. But remember; the truth sets you free. With God you can deal with anything. I remember her asking often "Will he ever love me again?"

I couldn't answer that. Only God knew what was in Steven's heart and where He was taking Steven. You see God is *always* faithful but there was no guarantee that Steven would obey God. But there IS the guarantee that God would honor Maggie's obedience regardless of what Steven did, even if it meant Steven would choose to leave, God would be Maggie's portion and that is better than any earthly blessing or human love.

It was a year later, the following February, that I received a phone call from Maggie early in the morning. She was obviously excited.

"Guess what?" She asked breathlessly.

"HE SAID IT DIDN'T HE?" I was almost in tears. I knew he had told her he loved her.

"Yes, he said he loves me." She was thrilled, shocked, overwhelmed. She had gotten into a comfortable pattern of following through with her role and emotionally distancing herself and not expecting anything from Steven, he was in God's hands. So trusting God and not looking for her own results she had simply faced each day waiting on God, not Steven. And BOOM – she is blown away. Somewhere in the middle of all this mess God had been working on

59

Steven and He didn't even need to let Maggie in on the details. Isn't God good?

Why do we think we need to know how God is going to work on our spouses. We don't even know what God might be teaching them. I was at a women's conference with the 1st Peter 3 girls and heard Bishop Wellington Boone's wife speak. She used the word picture of a woman taking her car to the mechanic to get repaired. What if the woman followed the mechanic into the garage and looking over his shoulder began to give him her opinion of what was wrong. 'I think that thingy over there is loose and you might want to check this valve thing over here and…' on and on. The mechanic would most likely say "Ma'am would you please go wait in the waiting area and let me do my job. I'll fix it and come and get you as soon as it's done."

We as wives need to get ourselves to God's waiting room and let the Master Mechanic work on our husbands. And trust me, He will let you know when He's done.

In the mean time, Lori was still plugging away. Dealing with the daily grind as Maggie had. I was so excited about what was happening in Maggie's life and shared the encouragement with Lori. But Lori's situation had been going on for years now with still no apparent change. It was time Maggie and Lori meet somehow. They needed each others support and friendship and Maggie had come up with the perfect solution.

They say that necessity is the mother of invention. Well we didn't invent email but our long distance phone bills certainly had created a necessity for *something*. Maggie's field is computers and being the practical woman that she is, she began to look into the possibility of email for us to try and decrease our soaring long distance bills. She found and installed a free email program on my computer and got us up and running and then I did the same for Lori. I introduced them by computer and we began to communicate daily by email, Lori and Maggie getting to know each other personally, sharing their testimonies', struggles, and personal victories directly.

It was a great idea. Our theme of course, being 1st Peter 3 and it was working.

In the coming weeks God would bring several more women into our lives and the 1st Peter 3 girls would begin to evolve into a vital ministry and life line for each of us.

CHAPTER TEN

"Send Me Lord!"

Maggie, Lori and I were on an emotional high for a while. Steven loved his wife again and was actively working on the marriage. Maggie didn't ask when he quit seeing the other woman, she just knew it had happened. She trusted God with the details. She didn't need to know.

Steven's attitude had obviously changed. During those months he would often apologize. Humble repentance. He was willing to be accountable. Were things perfect? No. They continued to work on healing the wounds in the relationship but God also orchestrates our lives and brings things along that help the healing. Steven had been asked by a friend to help with the music at a different church. He began to attend. Alone at first. This was a big step since they had been out of church for almost a year. Then he started asking Maggie if she and the girls would go along. Gradually, they began to attend regularly as a family. Once again being spiritually fed by biblical preaching and getting to know new people, the healing continued.

It was an exciting time for Maggie and for Lori and I as we watched God do this miracle. We kept up our communications often on e-mail, Maggie being a great source of encouragement for Lori, still struggling with her situation.

From the beginning of this saga, Maggie had looked for success stories. She wanted to hear from people who had obeyed scripture and then God had done miraculous things. She found that there was a lot of positive information out there but not a lot of people sharing real life success stories. Books like Boundaries and Love Must Be Tough were a great help and encouragement in giving her direction, but she *craved* success stories. Especially during the darkest times when people around her said there was no hope. She knew that God was faithful and she trusted His Word but wasn't there anyone who believed the same way and had lived it? Who wanted to share their testimony? Most of the Christians in her community, as I have said before, simply shook their heads and offered pity, not Biblical answers or encouragement. And there was not anyone close to her willing to invest themselves in her life.

The Bible calls us to lift one another up, not tear down. Philippians 4 talks about not worrying, always praying, and thinking on, for lack of a better word, positive things. Looking for God's best in a situation, not the world's failures. We need to remember as Christians that society's statistics *are not God's statistics.*

I remember Maggie telling God that she would use her story to help and encourage others. She knew what it was like to *need* to hear God's success stories. She just didn't know how soon He would ask her to step out of her comfort zone to share hers.

It had started with sharing with Lori on email. Then it wasn't long before God brought other women into Maggie's life at work who began to share with her their own personal struggles, opening a door for her to give her testimony.

You have to understand how far God had brought Maggie. Maggie is not a people person. She does not "do" crowds nor does she feel comfortable getting too personal with people she doesn't know well. Don't misunderstand me, she likes a good get together and enjoys group outings, but is intimidated to share personally in front of people. She relates best on a one-on-one level and God surely began using her in that capacity at work.

God also gave Lori the opportunity to share with a few women going through similar struggles. Even though Lori was still in the midst of seemingly impossible circumstances, she had grown in her faith and had a burden to share and encourage other women.

Christian men and women in lousy marriages. Pornography and adultery everywhere. It seemed they were coming out of the woodwork, in our community, in our work places, and shockingly in our own church. Were there any healthy, Godly marriages anymore? Are most people in church pretending? It sure felt that way after talking to woman after woman. The scenarios were becoming all too familiar. Similar problems, similar attitudes, most ending in divorce. Where were the older women teaching the younger women how to be godly wives? Where were the older men teaching the younger men how to be godly husbands? And where were the Christians wanting to just obey God's Word and be God's men and women no matter what the cost?

The more I heard the angrier I got. Not at the sin taking such a toll on the world, but at us, the Church, allowing sin to take such a devastating toll on our own. We've been given everything we need pertaining to life and Godliness and we still buy into the lie and allow Satan to ruin our effectiveness and witness in our communities as well as our lives and our effectiveness in passing God's heritage down to our children. Not to mention the books and literature and radio broadcasts offering sound Biblical guidance that are available to us and still we choose mediocrity.

It became blatantly obvious that a Biblical, 1st Peter 3 attitude was sorely lacking among Christian women who felt helpless and defeated and robbed of any joy in their relationships. Maybe the problem is we are flooded with great information and opportunities but in this age of technology we have less and less personal, accountable, intimate relationships. It's seems to all be superficial. You hear something you know applies to you but you have no one to talk with about it to help you sort it out and then hold you accountable to apply it to your own life. We are so busy we only have time for quick messages, meals on the go, answering machines, even email can become just an impersonal way of communicating. No commitment to invest ourselves in each others lives and share burdens, cry or laugh together, challenge each other, hold one another accountable to the Word, and worst of all, no time for personal, intimate time with God in prayer. It is far too easy today to skim over relationships on our way to the next event, or job, or church activity or just click delete and we don't have to face it anymore.

Maggie and Lori had told God to send them. Whatever He wanted, in their marriages and in their relationships with other women. We each had committed to be there for each other and hold each other accountable to God's Word, even if it hurt, knowing the outcome would be God's blessing regardless of the circumstance.

We were walking this journey together and in doing so God would give us sweet fellowship and strength and grow us in areas we never expected. He would also begin to bring others into each of our lives that would eventually be added to our group. It was an awesome thing to watch God work as He brought each woman to us through unique situations.

CHAPTER ELEVEN

Erica and Jeanie

Erica and Maggie had been friends since childhood. They attended high school and college together and Erica had been Maggie's maid of honor. They had kept in contact over the years and at one point Erica had even lived with Steven and Maggie for a time before they moved back home and Erica had married. Maggie and Erica still spoke on the phone periodically and Maggie had shared about the problems she and Steven were having and kept her updated on how things were going so Erica could support them in prayer.

It was great for Maggie to be able to share with Erica what God had been doing in her marriage and Erica became excited about the 1st Peter 3 concept. Erica, although married to a Christian man, still struggled with her role and responsibilities in marriage. There wasn't any critical situation at the time, just a mundane status quo. One that Erica wanted to overcome in her spiritual and personal life and she was eager to be a pro-active wife and mother but struggled with feelings of failure and insecurity.

So Maggie invited her to join us on email. Little did we know that some three years later Erica would find herself in a situation where she very much needed the support and encouragement of the 1P3 girls.

At the same time Lori had been getting to know another woman through the Mothers of Preschoolers ministry at our church. Lori had gotten involved in

MOPS because her youngest was still a preschooler and Jeanie had 2 small children. Jeanie and her husband Tim had been coming to our church for a while but neither Lori nor I knew her very well. Tim and Jeanie joined our Homebuilder's Sunday school class and Lori and Jeanie began to establish a friendship. Jeanie began to hint to Lori that she and her husband were having problems.

Because of the personal and sensitive nature of her own situation, Lori was very cautious about what she would share and to whom she would share it, but she felt God was leading her to open up with Jeanie.

Jeanie would eventually open her broken heart to Lori and share that her husband had an addiction to pornography and that she had found proof that he had had several adulterous relationships with women he had met on the Internet. Jeanie's life was falling apart. Should she leave him? Give him an ultimatum? She didn't know what to do but she wanted to save her family if at all possible and protect her children. The gut-wrenching part for Jeanie was that her husband, Tim, had been the one to lead her to Christ before they were married. She respected his walk with the Lord and never expected to end up here.

She would soon find out that Tim had been exposed to pornography as a young boy and had struggled with the problem before they met. She was not aware of this until after it had affected their marriage. She was blind-sided, much like Lori. That feeling of helplessness encompassed her. Was it inevitable that there was nothing she could do but watch her family fall apart and become another statistic? Should she wallow in the pain and betrayal, dump the bum and get on with her life?

Lori's response to her was to invite Jeanie to join us on email. Our group was growing and the women were hungry for real direction from God and a place they could go to share, vent, and work through the hurt and chaos of their lives.

I was overwhelmed at times by what was happening. Again, feeling like this was a huge issue in the church. How could this be? Marriages falling apart. Couples losing sight of who God had called them to be. How did we as a church get to the point that there was no difference statistically in the number of marriages that end in divorce? Do we have nothing to offer a hurting world? Where is the message of God's healing love and forgiveness? As a church, or even as individuals, what are we doing, or not doing that is obviously hindering us from responding to such a great need?

The Bible teaches that we are to be as wise as serpents yet as innocent as doves. If we do not recognize the danger signs we will wander in a wilderness of pain and disillusionment. The problem today is that we have allowed society to infiltrate our churches and attitudes. It is so subtle we don't even know it's there or what to look for. We have traded sharp, Biblical wisdom for a jaded skepticism and our innocence for blind ignorance. We choose to involve ourselves in things that rob us of our spiritual edge and then we close our eyes and choose to ignore blatant sin in our lives and in our churches. We compromise God's Word and his statutes and rationalize our sin.

Then, in order to maintain our rationalization of sin, we isolate ourselves from each other. We do not involve ourselves in the Body of Christ. Women and men are not risking personal involvement in teaching one another Biblical principles on a one-to-one basis and then holding each other accountable. It's too uncomfortable. We are too busy. It's none of our business. There are millions of excuses we give each other and tell ourselves, to make us feel better about disobeying God in this area.

We live in the age of information, where there is a wealth of good, Biblically sound, material at our fingertips. There are books, radio broadcasts, conferences, concerts as well as our local church programs. Promise Keepers is one of the most powerful movements of the Holy Spirit I have seen in recent years. God has truly given men in this country an opportunity to respond to His Holy call. I have listened to the speakers as they have been broadcast over the radio. I watched on television as a million men fell to their faces in repentance in Washington D.C. I was moved and humbled by God's power and the response of so many men. And even more so to know that my husband and son were there being touched by God at this historic event.

Yet with all this wealth of spiritual food, I am seeing in my community and my own church, people who are starving in their spiritual lives. They are in the middle of an oasis and they are dying of thirst and don't even know it.

Any woman who uses cosmetics knows that you can have a cabinet full of expensive make up and beauty tools but if you don't *apply* any of them, they are useless. I could have cupboards filled with beauty supplies but what if, every time someone came to see me, I answered the door not having washed or combed my hair for days, or bathed or washed my face for days, or used any of the products I so proudly owned. Then I would invite them in and brag about my stock pile of expensive cosmetics and show them all my wondrous beauty aids, they would look at me, and I mean *really* look at me, and think I was absolutely *out of my mind*. Why would I do that? Why would *you* do that? You see *application* is *critical*. Biblical principles have to be applied to work. And why don't we apply them? It takes too much work. I'm busy with other things. I'll do it later. I just *can't,* it's too hard. The excuses are limitless.

The path that marriages take if Biblical principles are not applied and the relationships are not maintained is devastating. There is a book by Dennis Rainey entitled Staying Close that addresses the issue of the natural drift toward isolation in marriage. Every marriage, left unattended, is drawn down this path. Once headed that way, unprotected, we are left open to Satan's attacks. Not being prepared, we find ourselves in an unknown, dangerous place, not knowing where to turn or what to do.

We do not frequently check our compass, the Bible, or we get our eyes of our Guide, the Lord, so we end up alone and scared usually in a panic and we make emotional, wrong decisions. And not having established intimate relationships in the Body of Christ we are not held accountable for applying those Biblical principles that will get us back on track. It becomes too easy to just wander in the wilderness and let life happen to you instead of having a map and making Biblical choices to struggle our way back to the straight and narrow, heading in the right direction.

The 1st Peter 3 group was becoming a place to take refuge. A rest area of sorts to regroup and take a look at the map once again and get our bearings and then head out together in this struggle to find our way back to God's straight and narrow as women.

Jeanie needed the kind of encouragement Lori, living it right along with her, could give her. She needed the hope that Maggie, having made it through to the other side of the tunnel, could give her. Erica would learn and grow by walking this path with these women, learning the stumbling blocks to avoid and becoming much more aware and wise in her own relationship with her husband. It would come to the point in Erica's life that she, also, would begin to recognize red flags where her husband was concerned and find that part of the reason for the spiritual apathy in their lives was due to a hidden addiction to pornography. Her husband, Tom, had struggled for years with this and she had had no idea. He had been exposed to pornography at a very young age, about 4th grade, and it had taken its toll on his life and had noticeably affected their marriage. Jeanie and Erica had similar stories, just at different times in our journey together. God in His infinite wisdom had again known what we would need and when, and had choreographed our lives to bring us together at just the right time.

And I would spend my time with them going over scripture after scripture and we would pray for direction for each of us to apply it to our own lives and marriages. Their choices and faith would strengthen my own faith and resolve to be a godly woman and a 1st Peter 3 wife.

Soon there would be two more joining Lori, Maggie, Erica, Jeanie, and I on this journey.

God would add so much more to our group by bringing us different perspectives and spiritual gifts to encourage one another and, through His Word, would continue to bind us together in a way that transcends ordinary human relationships.

CHAPTER TWELVE

Mandy and Julia

Life with God is an adventure and sometimes His surprises make me smile with joy.

The way things began to snowball with the 1st Peter 3 girls was definitely exciting but watching the girls grow and reach out to others was the most rewarding for me. If someone would have told Maggie a year before that not only would her marriage be healed and growing, but that she would be willingly stepping out of her comfort zone and sharing with other women at her work place, she would have flat out said they were crazy. Ok I *did* tell her that and I loved being able to say, "I told you so". It was so much fun to watch unfold.

Maggie had called me all excited that she had begun to spend time with Mandy, a girl at her work, and had had the opportunity to share with her her testimony of what God had done in her marriage. One thing had lead to another and as they talked, Maggie learned that Mandy had been raised with some exposure to church but had not accepted Christ's gift of salvation. She also learned that Mandy was engaged to a young man named Bill who was also not a Christian. They had been living together and were planning on getting married in the next few months.

Maggie and Mandy talked daily and as their friendship grew, Maggie invited them to visit their church. Mandy was young, about 24 years old, and very eager to learn about the God that had done such miracles in Maggie's life. After attending a service with Steven and Maggie, one of the pastor's visited Mandy and Bill at home later in the week, and they both made a decision to accept God's gift of forgiveness and salvation. Talk about exciting. We were all ecstatic. Maggie had shared with the 1st Peter 3 girls after she had begun talking with Mandy and we had been praying for Mandy and Bill for weeks. Mandy was hungry for more. She wanted to join the group. What better time to learn about being a godly wife than before you walked down the isle?

She and Bill attended a Family Life Marriage conference and as a result made a commitment to purity and to stay away from each other physically until their wedding, which was a huge step since they had been living together for a couple of years. They received a purity contract at the conference that they signed and kept and Mandy asked the 1st Peter 3 girls to keep her accountable to that commitment. It was so exciting to be a part of their spiritual growth.

Also during this time Maggie was getting to know another woman at work, Julia. As they began to get better acquainted, Julia shared that her husband, Kent had been invited to a Promise Keepers conference a couple of years before and had come home excited and shared with her his new found faith and relationship with Jesus Christ. As a result of his sharing with her, Julia also accepted God's gift of salvation. They had been learning and growing in their walk with the Lord and, as a fairly new believer, she was interested in becoming involved in the 1st Peter 3 group. Julia became, and still is, our cheerleader. She always has a positive word of encouragement and an 'Amen' when needed.

As our relationships developed, some of our husbands began to take an active, positive supportive role with the group as they began to see the spiritual benefits in the lives of their wives and in turn their own. Kent and my husband Len would be great resources for us for prayer, leadership, and Biblical advice from a man's perspective, when needed. Kent is a wonderful, godly man, who has taken his spiritual leadership role very seriously in their marriage and together, he and Julia have become our prayer warriors.

And as for my husband, Len, I will share about him later on but I am thankful for a godly husband who also believes God's Word and acts on it.

Mandy and Julia were an exciting addition to our little group. Julia with her quiet grace and encouragement and Mandy with her infectious spirit and humor. Mandy had just begun to walk the path of a godly woman and would have some serious struggles with her own spiritual growth and in her relationship with Bill after their marriage. But with God's direction and the encouragement of the 1st Peter 3 girls she would learn some basic Biblical principles that would eventually become a reality in her life and be the foundation for real growth and change later on.

Our little group wasn't so little anymore and God was getting ready to add two more women during this same time.

CHAPTER THIRTEEN

Renee and Stacy

Renee and Brian were our neighbors. I remember when they moved in several years before. Their dog had gotten loose and Brian had come over to get him and we chatted for a few moments, getting acquainted. As we talked I mentioned our church and extended an open invitation. Brian immediately suggested that I not say anything to his wife, Renee, about church. It seemed she had been deeply hurt by an experience in her teens when the church she and her sister attended had split. As a teenager, not having come from a Christian home and looking for the love and acceptance she had been told God offered, she became very disillusioned by the hypocrisy she witnessed and bitterly turned her back on the church, feeling she could worship God alone. She didn't need so called "Christians".

Renee had been through a lot in the 20 years since that time. This was the second marriage for both Brian and Renee. Her first marriage to an alcoholic had ended in divorce when he became abusive. Raising two small children alone, she had joined the Air National Guard to support her family and there met Brian. Having just gone through a divorce himself and with one young son, the two of them shared common experiences and pain. They married and shortly after moved into our neighborhood.

You know, when Brian advised me not to broach the subject of church or God with Renee, I took that as a challenge. I wanted to show this woman God's love and that we are not all perfect but that God does use Christians in the Body and He does forgive and heal.

When I did finally meet Renee, we hit it off right away. We spent hours talking about life and she shared what she had been through. I was amazed at how strong this woman was but I knew that she needed God's healing touch in her life. Through our friendship she and her children began attending church with us and she rededicated her life to Christ.

Then things began to fall apart. Brian had had some exposure to church and Christianity and said he had made a profession of faith as a young boy but also had not been in church in years and did not seem interested in spiritual things. Things had been strained in their marriage almost from the beginning. Even only being married a short time they had both come into the relationship with a lot of baggage and hurt and it was affecting the marriage.

When a woman has been through what Renee had, she tends to crave love and security. Security then becomes a control issue. If I can control the other person or the situation I won't be hurt again. The more we try to control the more we lose control. The more the other person withdraws. The more insecure we get. It is a vicious cycle that was beginning to be repeated in their lives.

Renee discovered Brian was seeing another woman. Now what? Does the same principle apply here that does for Maggie and Lori and Jeanie? Of course. But it doesn't make it any easier. Renee had some 1st Peter 3 issues to deal with just like the rest of us. It was time to shut up.

The "without a word" issue was the reoccurring theme in each of our lives as women. Why is it so hard for us to give up control? To shut our mouths? To take God at His word and just do it?

*Prov. 14:1 "The wise woman builds her house, but with **her own hands** the foolish one tears hers down." NIV*

I believe as women we use our tongues as tools to foolishly tear our own houses down and we don't even realize it. We criticize, ridicule, and emasculate our husbands with our words and then wonder why they refuse to take the leadership role in marriage and don't love us the way we need to be loved. We use our tongues and stand between God and our husbands and become stumbling blocks they trip over and we still continue to kick and stab them while they are down.

Well, as with the rest of us, Renee had to deal with this area in her life. She needed to recognize her own patterns and turn them over to God and then begin to change. Not to change the circumstances, but to become who God wanted her to be regardless of the outcome.

We had been friends for a couple of years at this point and Renee had become friends with Lori through church and knew about Maggie and our 1st Peter 3 group but had only recently been able to join us on line. It became a great encouragement to her to know there were other women out there supporting her Biblical choices and praying for her and each other. Brian did come to a point where he chose to stay in the marriage and has participated in church to some extent, but has yet to really commit his life to Christ wholeheartedly. It is one of the things we continue to pray for.

But Renee has a gift for communicating clearly and, even being in a difficult situation herself, her insights have been very discerning.

So adding Renee to our band of merry women, we continued to grow.

Another day, another phone call. This time from a long time childhood friend I hadn't heard from in a few years. Stacy and I grew up together in church. My father was her pastor and she and her sister were my close friends. As adults Len and I had spent time together with Stacy and her husband Greg early in our marriage relationships. But they had started a family before we did and then moved to a small community out of town and we didn't see much of them other than occasionally. We still had a great time when we got together but had moved on to different stages in our lives over the years.

This particular day Stacy had seen someone we both had grown up with and thought of me and decided to call. It was fun catching up and we made plans for all of us to get together. So we did a couple of times over the ensuing months, getting to know their children, Jill, now 19 and Dave, 16 and enjoying the fellowship.

I had always respected Stacy and Greg's marriage and their commitment to the Lord and His Word. I still did. They had raised their children in a loving, Christian home. They had gone to the Family Life seminars, heard Josh McDowell speak, and bought all the "right" books on Christian parenting and marriage. They had lived a godly example of marriage in front of their children. They weren't perfect in their humanness but they were definitely committed to God's will in their family.

Then, shortly after we had begun to spend time with them again, Stacy called crying. She was devastated. Jill, their 19 year old daughter, had moved out without warning and cut off communication with her parents. For several weeks she had been acting different and seemed to become a totally different person before their eyes. And then, arriving home from church on a Sunday afternoon, they found her things gone. She had moved out. They didn't know where to find her or how to contact her. They were frantic with worry. This wasn't at all like the Jen they knew. When they finally did locate her, it wasn't their Jill. It was a cruel joke. This Jill was living in a less than desirable atmosphere. Rumors were that she was drinking, smoking, partying and even doing drugs. She didn't bother denying it. But she did begin a pattern of lying about things. She wouldn't be where she said she would be. She walked out on her job and college. She would avoid talking with them at all and have her friends lie to them about her.

Stacy was beside herself with grief and worry. How could this happen? She would call Jill's friends and try to talk to them about what was going on. She would track Jill down and try to talk to her, asking her "why" and begging for Jill to tell her what had happened. The more she tried, the more distant and evasive Jill became. The more she shut them out. She wanted nothing more to do with church and God or her family. It was mind-boggling. What was a mother to do?

Listening to Stacy share her heartbrokenness I began to wonder if the 1st Peter 3 concept would apply in this situation. Stacy surely could use the encouragement of other wives and mothers and the prayer support. So I invited her to join us. It is amazing to me how universal God's principles are. As I've said before, human nature is human nature, and sin is sin. Jill was doing the same thing in running from God and Stacy needed to let go and give her daughter to Him. She could no longer be a mother to her daughter. Jill was an adult and making choices on her own. Stacy could not control Jill or the circumstances. For a mother, letting go, especially in a situation like this, is the hardest thing to do. But she needed to shut up, get on her knees, and let God take over.

So, she too became a 1st Peter 3 girl. It was amazing how similar the emotional pain was to those women dealing with marital issues. We had a lot in common. All women, wanting to be who God called us to be, fighting spiritual battles and dealing with our own human frailties. What a combination of women and, together, what a powerful force in the spiritual battles God had called us fight.

Before I go back and share with you what eventually happened in Lori's life, I want to introduce you to the most recent member of our original 1st Peter 3 group. Traci.

CHAPTER FOURTEEN

Traci

It was my daughter's 12th birthday and we were taking her to a Grover Levy concert at a local Bible Conference Center. There were hundreds of teens and adults everywhere, getting their seats and talking with friends. I turned around in my seat looking over the auditorium for people I knew and there was Traci, walking directly toward me. I hadn't seen her in more than 15 years. We had been best friends in Jr. High but then in high school we went in different directions. She began making choices that led her away from church and God and we became like distant acquaintances.

After graduating she married Kyle, a non-Christian guy we had gone to school with, and after joining the military, eventually they moved away. I had seen her only briefly, once or twice in the first couple of years before they left the states for Germany. I had also married but Traci and I didn't seem to have much in common.

I remember one time talking with her about the Lord and I'll never forget when she said, almost with regret, "I wish I could be like you". It was a humbling statement that I wasn't comfortable with and I didn't understand then that Traci had been and would for years continue to struggle with understanding God's grace and forgiveness in her life. I would occasionally see her mother and ask how she was doing and in recent years had heard that they had moved back to the states and she had gotten back into church.

Then here she was, walking straight at me. I was so excited to see her. She looked great. She and her sister sat next to us and we tried to catch up before the concert began. We talked about our upcoming high school class reunion and I asked if she and Kyle would be attending. She seemed rather uncomfortable at first and then told me that Kyle had left her just three weeks before. She had gone to a Christian women's conference and upon returning had found he had moved out without explanation.

Another tragic story. Another open door for God to work and use the 1st Peter 3 girls. Of course I shared with her a little about the group and also found she was looking for a part time job. I had been working as a lunch room supervisor at a local junior high and knew we were needing another person to join the team so I gave her the information and the next Monday she showed up and went to work. We were able to get re-acquainted working together every day and as she shared more details about her life and marriage it began to sound sadly familiar.

Traci is a shy person and was hesitant about joining a group of women and sharing her personal struggles with strangers. But she eventually did join us and as each woman shared her own story Traci began to understand that she was not alone. It took her the better part of a year to really be able to open up and be honest about her feelings and what God was doing in her life.

But it was an exciting time for us as a group. Traci had joined us just after things had started to get interesting in Lori's life again. Remember how devastating it had been to learn the truth about Dan? Well over 7 years later Lori was still plugging away being a 1st Peter 3 wife living with a husband who was living a lie, when things began to intensify in their home.

CHAPTER FIFTEEN

The Dark Before Dawn

Seven years had now passed since we had learned Dan's devastating secret. And for seven years Lori had been living with pain, frustration, and disillusionment. But she had also been living with something else. Hope. Her faith in the Lord had grown tremendously. She was able to counsel and share with women in similar situations, encouraging them in their relationship with the Lord even though she lived daily with a humanly unbearable situation. It was a powerful message.

Lori had done a lot of changing in those seven years. She had learned to set boundaries and not eat that plate of food that Dan would daily sit before her. She had begun to learn how to recognize the false guilt and not be controlled by it. She was learning to listen to the still, small voice of the Holy Spirit in her life through the Word, prayer and obedience. It had not been over night nor was it easy. But little by little, as she turned her heartache and sorrow over to the Lord, he began to show Himself very real to her. God became her portion. Regardless of her husband, and his choices. She had come to the point that no matter if Dan never chose to submit himself to the Lord, she would and would trust her savior to meet her needs and sustain her. This is critical in our relationship to the Lord. He is not the sugar daddy in the sky, giving us everything we want, when we want it. He is our loving Heavenly Father who knows us better than we know ourselves. He knows our frailties and shortcomings. And He also sees where He is taking us and if we realize that it is a better place than we can imagine and that the purpose of our lives is not to be *happy* but to be *one with Him*, then we can have *true* peace and inner joy.

Reaching this point did not mean that she did not have doubts to struggle with. She would grow tired at times. Emotionally drained. She dealt with loneliness and temptation. And even at one point, considered a relationship with a man who had been pursuing her. Seven years of living in an emotional desert, devoid of love and intimacy, for a moment she saw a mirage.

This man and his wife were attending our church at the time. Lori and Dan and this gentleman and his wife had gotten acquainted through, of all things, a Homebuilders marriage study with several other couples. The man had shared some of the struggles he and his wife were having. He seemed to pour his heart out and be very sensitive. They had gone to counseling and were working on their marriage, his wife was very quiet and at times, very skeptical.

Dan and Lori had gotten together with them socially a few times and had shared a few of the details of their marriage struggles but not the true heart of what they were going through. Dan connected with the man and they became friends. Dan seemed to identify with the other man's weaknesses.

The man had struggled for years with infidelity and possibly pornography. The chase and conquering of women had become an addiction. He had gone to all the right counselors and seminars. Had been in accountability groups. The whole nine yards. And he had learned to jump through those hoops. He could say it with the best of them. But it wasn't real from the inside out. A professed believer, living a lie. Just like Dan.

He had gotten into another adulterous relationship and his wife had asked him to leave. He left his family and after a time went through the motions of repentance and again came back to church. And all the while maintaining a superficial friendship with Dan and Lori.

A few of us from our church had signed up to work at youth camp that summer and he was included in the group. He and Dan spent quite a bit of time together becoming even closer. Dan was sharing things about his feelings and the other man would seem to listen and empathize. Then he began to manipulate Dan and their friendship. But of course, Dan was using him to feel better about himself also. It was a very dysfunctional and dangerous game. He became Dan's best friend and began calling the house for Dan, when Dan wasn't home, and then would spend time talking with Lori. He was very subtle at first. All the while zeroing in on her weaknesses. Then he began crossing lines into inappropriate intimate conversation. Talking to her as a woman, not as his friend's wife, and telling her how beautiful she was and what a fool Dan was. It didn't take long to go from bad to worse. He began calling her frequently and for a woman who had not felt loved or wanted as a woman by her own husband for over seven years, it felt wonderful.

But what Dan had done did not give Lori the right to disobey God and she knew it. It had only gone on for a matter of weeks but it had escalated and the man wanted her to meet him somewhere. Lori knew she was in over her head. She had kept this from everyone, including the 1st Peter 3 girls. At first, instead of cutting off the relationship entirely, she would reason with him. They shouldn't be doing this. It wasn't right. He would agree, of course. He even suggested that both Lori and he get together with Len and I for accountability.

Is Satan crafty or what?

Lori knew what she had to do and it wasn't easy. She had crossed a line out of her weakness and for a moment it felt good. But then reality set in. The Bible teaches that there is pleasure in sin for a season but the ultimate penalty is not worth the price not to mention broken fellowship with our Savior. The question for Lori again became, 'Is God who He says He is' and 'Do I believe He will honor His Word and meet my needs?'.

She made a decision. She would not meet him anywhere and she made another phone call. Lori called me and asked if I'd go to lunch with her. She wanted to talk. There was nothing unusual about her request but she was acting a little odd. Sitting in the parking lot of a local shopping center she said she had something she wanted to tell me and then she wanted me to hold her accountable.

"Ok." I said; not having any idea what was coming.

Then she began to tell me that there was a man pursuing her and she was having trouble resisting. I knew immediately who it was and she confirmed it. She was very upset and knew even the phone conversations she'd had with him had been wrong. This was *real* guilt, conviction from the Holy Spirit, and Lori was giving up her will and doing the right thing. I don't know how long we sat in the car with Lori pouring out her heart and crying but it was a time of cleansing for her. We decided that she would not talk to him under any circumstances, except to tell him to never call her again the next time he called. She would not even initiate a call to end it. I was not sure what to tell her about how to handle it with Dan. She had not actually seen the man alone. Their inappropriate relationship had been carried out on the phone, but should she confess her sin to Dan and ask his forgiveness?

The world would tell Lori that she had done nothing to be forgiven for. But according to God's Word she knew she had sinned against God and her husband. Even if Dan did not deserve it, Lori's commitment was before God. We would have to pray about it and I would agree to tell my husband, Len, and ask him for his perspective and counsel in this situation. At first I was leaning toward not telling Dan. What would the purpose be? But Len, with the Holy Spirit's prompting I believe, advised her that she tell Dan what had happened. This was a man who had used Dan to get to his wife. This was about more than just Lori.

It was the next day, I believe, that she told Dan what had been happening and asked for his forgiveness. It came as a shock to Dan. A friend had betrayed him. Actually, the man had done to Dan what Dan had been doing to people for 30 some years. Lying and deception, using people to get what he wanted regardless of what it did to them. He was angry. He actually said to Lori "This is me isn't it? This is how I am."

Dan was forced to recognize the harsh reality of what he was by being on the receiving end. He was hurt, but not enough to repent and give up his sin. He was actually more upset by the fact that the *man* had betrayed him rather than Lori. Self-pity for certain, and possibly even self-loathing became Dan's banner. He became bitter and nursed a hatred for the man. He withdrew even further from his marriage and anyone who really loved and cared about him.

Lori had also shared her struggle with this temptation with the 1st Peter 3 girls and through prayer, support, and accountability had totally cut off any contact with the man. This seemed to be another turning point for Lori in her walk with the Lord. She became more focused and sensitive to the Holy Spirit's direction in her life.

She would need this in the coming months because things were soon to take a turn for the worst.

Shortly after this my husband, Len, and I sat down with Dan and Lori for a frank discussion of where they were in their marriage. My husband was serving as their deacon in the church at the time and felt a responsibility to both of them to continue to pursue them spiritually.

I remember being angry with Dan. It had been such a long battle and after everything, still no change. I had to deal with my own feelings of resentment. We had all been friends such a long time and he had lied to all of us. I did not believe anything he said at this point and was struggling with submission to my husbands wisdom in even sitting down to discuss anything with them as a couple.

But God is gracious and in His wisdom was leading Len in his spiritual role. Len had come with specific questions to ask them both and expected answers. He is very gentle in his manner, which, in my opinion, made him an effective deacon. In hindsight, I believe part of God's directing Len to ask these questions and have Dan and Lori both answer was a step in holding them accountable before Him. If either of them would lie, they would then have to own the consequences. There would be no shifting blame.

Len had selected several verses of scripture to read regarding the marriage commitment. After reading he looked each of them in the eye and asked them if they had a personal relationship with Christ. Were they saved? Each of them answered "yes". I was really struggling at this point with Dan's attitude and response. I was giving in to an ungodly attitude and began to make sarcastic comments. My wonderful husband, in his wisdom, told me to be quiet. Amazingly, I did. He advised me, in front of them both, that I had to take Dan's word at face value, I did not have a right to judge motive at this point.

He then asked them individually if they were willing to do whatever it took to heal their marriage and fulfill their God given roles in marriage. Again, they both answered "yes". Dan said he was willing to do whatever God asked him to do.

At some point after that, we spoke of our relationship as friends. I was honest with Dan about the hurt I felt and that it was hard for me to believe him. But that I would take him at his word, he was now accountable to God for his commitment made in front of us all. We prayed with them and everyone hugged and we left.

Still in my spirit I knew Dan wasn't there yet. But as my husband said, I had to leave it with God. It was His responsibility. There was nothing more to do but pray. You see Dan was still "doing" all the right things. There was nothing to "prove" the sin that was going on in his life, no facts to point to. But Lori knew. She lived with him.

Things went fairly smoothly for about two weeks. Which is about how long Dan would always try in his own strength to jump the hoops. Then it began all over again. I remember telling Lori; "You will know when he gets it right with God. You won't have to guess or wonder. It will be life changing for him." Lori had learned not to build her hopes on Dan. He had good days and bad. In the beginning she had focused on Dan and if he had a good day, she would think he was changing, then when it didn't last she would be hurt once again. She was past that now. At times it may seem cynical to not trust someone, but if we are fixing our gaze on Jesus and not our imperfect spouses or others, love truly does cover a multitude of sin and God can be trusted at all times.

In the next few months, Dan began to step up the charade. He became more and more verbally critical of others. Finding flaws in anyone who seemed to be genuinely walking the Christian walk. He loved gossip. It seemed to make him feel better about himself to hear other Christian's "dirty laundry".

Lori was feeling more and more like she had been sucked into this lie he was living and felt convicted about the charade. Having not had any kind of consistent physical relationship with Dan, more than several times a year, she began to feel convicted about sharing a bed with him. To everyone visiting their home, seeing their room, most people assumed they had a normal marriage relationship. This was one area that others did not ask about. It usually isn't anyone's business. But it was one area she felt strongest about. It was the area that most showed the symptoms of his sin.

Lori had called me and discussed taking radical action. She felt that she should move Dan out of their room. No matter how she had begged, asked, pleaded and reasoned with Dan, he had refused a physical relationship with her. It had been over 6 or 7 months by this time since he had last "forced" himself to be intimate with her. If this was his choice then she did not want to live a lie and have it look like things were normal. It made her feel as if she was helping him in his deception.

We talked about it and prayed about it. If she felt that this is what God wanted her to do, then she needed to do it. While Dan was at work, Lori moved his things to a bedroom in their basement. They had finished their basement with a bathroom, bedrooms and living area and lots of windows. It was a very pleasant atmosphere. She made his bed and hung his clothes. She did not do any of it out of anger. She had just drawn a significant boundary.

When he came home and found his things moved he became *very* angry. She was prepared for this and she stood her ground. She calmly explained that she felt that this is what God wanted her to do and that

God would make it clear to her when the situation would change.

Usually Dan would mask his anger in passive aggressive behavior but as God turned up the heat on Dan it was becoming more and more difficult for him to play the game, he was losing control and could not get Lori to eat that nasty food he had fixed. He told her "I am NOT sleeping in that basement." And then he left.

He was gone for over 24hours and she did not know where he was or if he was coming back. Part of the pattern of self-indulgence and sin in Dan's life showed itself in finances. He is a professional and makes a good income but there was never enough money. They had a brand new home he had wanted and two car payments. Because of her past, security was a big deal to Lori and when they married she had saved a considerable sum of money herself. Upon marrying Dan she paid off thousands of dollars in credit card debt, she paid the large down payment on the first house he wanted and even had had to pay for her own wedding band. Sin eventually shows up and takes its toll on every area of our lives.

Dan knew that Lori was frugal and that security was a big deal to her. That is why, 24hours later, Dan came home driving a brand new, $28,000 truck that he had been wanting for years that Lori had been saying they couldn't afford. Not only was Lori living without love and affection, he had now taken away any security that she had. This was a huge spiritual test for Lori.

She called me weeping. Lori is another very strong woman, not given easily to tears. As a nurse she sees a lot of suffering and gentle but also very practical. She had handled a lot of things in her life but this one, after everything she had been through, seemed to break her. Dan had hit her hard in the last vulnerable area for Lori.

Concerned, I immediately got off the phone and shared with Len what was going on. Len said, "Go get her." I immediately left and went to her home. She answered the door still weeping, Dan in the background ignoring her. I didn't even go in. I just told her, "Come on, we're going for a drive." At this point none of us could do a thing for Dan. Everything had been said. He had been confronted. God would deal with him. Lori needed the support of The Body more than ever.

We drove and then we parked and talked and cried and prayed. She could do this. This was another step of Lori getting out of the way and letting God work. Most people would have said "divorce him while you still can get something out of him. Take your kids and leave."

But no, that's not what God had in mind. Is God *really* who He says He is? Is the Bible *really* true? These questions need to be answered on a *daily* basis in our lives as we face whatever trials come because the answer will determine your response to those situations. If, as Christians, we do not ask ourselves and answer these based upon God's Word, then life merely just happens to us with no purpose and we do not see God's hand working. Then we become complacent, hopeless, depressed, living mediocre, benign, ineffective lives, accomplishing nothing for Christ and living without His peace and joy.

Humanly Lori was hurt, but spiritually she began to soar. She regrouped and went home to face her mountain. Time again to shut up and leave it at the altar.

Dan became angrier and more unpleasant to be around. Unable to maintain the façade as in the past, he became belligerent to her and the kids. Weekends became unbearable around him so Lori would take the kids and go for drives, take them for treats or visit friends. Dan continued to sleep in the basement no longer able to maintain that lie. He was left alone with his sin and his anger. Anger toward God and all of us. But Lori had given it up to God. The truck and her security, Dan, her pain and her children living in the midst of this chaos.

Dan, for the first time was truly alone, just Dan and God. No one standing between. No one to blame. Not his parents, or his wife, or his job, or his friends. *"It is a dreadful thing to fall into the hands of the living God." Heb. 10:31 NIV*

But after the terrible dark, there comes the glorious dawning...

CHAPTER SIXTEEN

The Dawning

It had been November when Lori moved Dan to the basement and he had then come home with the truck. Needless to say, it had not been a great holiday season for any of them. But God was working.

Dan did not have the money to make his first two payments on his new truck. He had leased it and half-heartedly attempted to get out of the lease to no avail. The financial pressure was mounting. Making the payments two months late left them without grocery money for that month. Still angry, he was forced to get a second job. He took a job at a local pizza restaurant. A humbling experience for a professional. But it was his decision and his problem to fix.

Lori had, several years before, quit her full time nursing job feeling that God wanted her home with her children, especially with the problems in their marriage. She was on a casual status at the hospital and would only work a couple days per month. This money she gave to Dan but it was not enough either. She also decided to not give him the child support money after prayerful consideration, feeling that it was money for her children's welfare and needs and began using some of it to feed them even if there was nothing in the house to fix that Dan had provided.

This, of course, made Dan furious. But in all of this, Lori kept a level head. It was, after all, Dan's job before the Lord to provide for his family and for Lori to usurp his position would be to sin. This is another area we, as women, tend to go astray. We think that if our husbands are not doing their jobs before the Lord and fulfilling their Biblical roles, then *somebody* has to do it, right? I *have* to because no one else will.

Wrong. This is where trusting the Lord becomes reality. God IS big enough to care for your needs and see that you are taken care of even if your husband is not following God's will and *without your taking over!* Again, this is such a difficult concept for women to grasp. Let go. Do *your* job, not his.

Lori refused to take control and do Dan's job for him. Dan began to bear the full brunt of the responsibility for his family and the pressure of the poor decisions he had been making financially. Interestingly enough, this, and not the homosexual issue, would be part of what God would use in Dan's life to finally get his attention.

As I have mentioned before, it wasn't really about homosexuality, or finances, or adultery. Those are just symptom sins, as I like to call them. The real issue is a deeper spiritual one. Rebellion against God and His will for your life. It is, as I have said before, a control issue. And this sin manifests itself in so many different ways in different people.

As this personal pressure grew, the Lord also turned the heat up at church. I cannot even remember what the sermons were about during this time. All I know is that we would all sit in church and listen and wonder how anyone could resist such a strong pull of the Holy Spirit. I would pray during each service for Dan, that God would get a hold of him and break and heal him.

Dan began to react physically after a while. He would fidget, not being able to sit still. His neck and face would turn beet red. And still he resisted. Finally, he started staying home for one reason or another. He was sick, or had a headache or was just too tired. This went on for a while but the very things he had committed to do in church that made him look good were the very things he had to force himself to go do now. Play the piano or sing in the choir. He could only miss so much without causing questions, which he obviously did not want to answer.

Not every church has altar calls nor do I believe that going forward is necessary to talk with God or make spiritual decisions, but Dan had said before that he *did not* have to go forward to get right with God. No, God does not require that of us but if He asks us to we should be willing to do whatever he asks. Dan had basically decided he *would not* do that. Pride. Plain and simple.

My mother used to tell me "Don't drive your stakes because God will make you pull them up." Her mother had told her and she told me. Wise advise. How dare we *tell God* what we will and will not do. We become arrogant in our own thinking and then it becomes an issue of submission and rebellion. The Bible tells us that *obedience is better than sacrifice.* What a difficult thing for us, as prideful humans, to learn. To rely on God's Grace, not our own finite idea of what God expects.

It was a Sunday in late April, just before Dan and Lori's 8th wedding anniversary. The sermon was about being an authentic Christian, not pretending. It was powerful to say the least. Len and I were sitting behind

Dan and Lori and again I was praying. But by this time my prayers were humanly mixed with doubt. Would he ever submit to the Holy Spirit? Or would we go on like this forever.

At the end of the service Pastor was down front extending the invitation and we were singing when Dan stepped out of the pew. I began to shake. Len began to cry. All I could see was the back of Lori and wasn't sure what she was feeling. As Dan got to the altar he spoke with pastor then sat down and began to pray. As we stopped singing, pastor said that Dan wanted to share with the congregation that he had been pretending a very long time and wanted Jesus to be Lord of ALL of his life.

I couldn't stop shaking. As soon as the service ended Len headed down toward Dan and Dan was practically running back toward us, bawling. Sobbing like I've never seen him do before. This was real. He and Len met half way and embraced and cried together. Then as he reached the pew I was in, he grabbed me crying and saying over and over "I'm so sorry, I'm so sorry". At that moment I knew God had done a great thing. All my anger and frustration was no longer a struggle. It was gone instantaneously. God makes it easy to forgive the pain in light of who He is and what He has done for, not just Dan, but me also. This was more than real; it was a divine change. Dan had submitted to God and God had freely given Dan the grace and forgiveness He had died on the cross to give. He had been waiting on Dan for 37 years.

It appeared that Dan and Lori weren't sure of what to do with each other at church. Their reunion would need to be a private one. At home they would again cry and hold each other and begin the long road back from pain and devastation to healing and restoration.

"If we confess our sins, he is faithful and just and will forgive us our sins and purify us from all unrighteousness." 1John 1:9 NIV

From that moment on, Dan has been a different person. Literally. I cannot even describe to you the changes in not only his attitude, but also even his appearance. It is with great joy that I write this. I remember when we celebrated the year anniversary of, as Dan puts it, "when I got my head on", it was a great milestone for all of us.

Sure Dan will struggle with the patterns in his life that had been so prevalent, and looking back over the last few years he has been seriously tested at times. But he has, and will continue to, struggle *through* them and not stagnate and die in them as he chooses to make Jesus Lord of his life. I truly respect Dan's walk with the Lord. Dan has even felt God's leading toward some type of ministry work. It amazes me what God can do with a life that everyone else has given up on.

Had Lori given up on Dan and, more importantly, on God, she would have been through her second divorce with children from both marriages not having a godly father and Dan, well I don't know where Dan would be. Missing out on the miracle and blessing God had for him, I'm sure.

Was it worth eight years of what everyone else viewed as a living hell?

What do you think?

God is still taking each of us in the 1st Peter 3 group through trials and the daily grind as human beings. The Lori and Maggie stories are the great mountain top experiences, but what about the rest of the time? What about the other girls, what other struggles did we and do we face together? What are the other victories we share in our lives as we walk together, striving to be God's women?

We are, after all, ordinary women leading ordinary lives, just like you. Or does God transform the ordinary into extraordinary for anyone who believes?

CHAPTER SEVENTEEN

Ordinary Lives - Extraordinary Women

In the course of years we have been a "group", we have each gone through many changes and struggles together. Each of us learning from each other and supporting each other in prayer.

Sex would often be a topic we would need to deal frankly with. Dealing with our attitudes toward our husbands in this area and with what the Bible required of us as wives was high on our list of discussions. This is a subject that we would all have input on and need to grow in.

Although I do not think it is necessarily appropriate to talk about certain specifics of your intimate life with your husband in a group setting like this, I do think that women need to work through some issue in this area. They need to know that they are not dysfunctional and not assume there is something wrong with them. We, as women, need to know that we share a common struggle with each other. There are some wonderful books out there on the subject but it is so great to have dialogue with other women about our fears and insecurities. We can learn so much from each other and in turn encourage each other to reach for the prize God has for us, even in this sensitive area.

Each of the 1st Peter 3 girls would need to lean on the rest at different times and stages of their lives and marriages.

ERICA

Erica, Maggie's friend since childhood, would initially struggle with the issue of taking on work and the stress of balancing it all with children while still being a Godly wife and sharing intimacy with her husband. We *all* struggled in this area. But this was the area that lead to her taking a personal inventory and being challenged by the other women in the group lead to a wake up call to the trouble signs with Tom. She had shared her concern for her seemingly lack of physical drive and knew that she needed accountability in dealing with this area of her life. Having set some personal goals for herself to improve her attitude toward sexual intimacy with her husband, she spent a year working on this and had personally improved. But then, having listened to the other women who were dealing with pornography in their marriages share some of the signs and situations they had gone through she began asking some very general questions about men and pornography. She eventually discovered what she, in the back of her mind, had been dreading. Initially she did not want to admit that it was a problem. Asking questions like "How do you know when it is an addiction and not just an occasional thing?"

How Satan does try to deceive us. There is no such thing as occasional willful sin. It is *always* a "must deal with" problem. After challenging Erica to take a hard, honest look at her life and her marriage, we encouraged her to confront Tom with boundaries. This was extremely out of character for Erica. *Way* out of her comfort zone. Tom was initially defensive and embarrassed. He knew the "girls" knew. But the Bible says, "be sure your sin will find you out". We truly felt badly for Tom and Erica both but knew this was the cleansing that needed to happen in their lives for God to heal their lives spiritually and in their marriage.

I remember my mother saying once that sometimes people need to be hurt before they can be healed. This is so true in our lives as Christians. It is painful at times to have the Great Physician cut the cancer out of our lives but after the surgery, we heal and go on to live fuller, abundant lives in Him.

It was only a matter of days after Erica confronted Tom with what she suspected and drew her boundaries before he totally surrendered it all to the Lord. They had a time of weeping and praying together on their living room floor. A time of forgiveness and healing and intimacy they had never experienced before.

It still amazes me how intricately God weaves the patterns of our lives. Not leaving any thread undone. Tom went to work and through a conversation with a fellow believer that very week, found that he was not alone in his struggles and the co-worker invited him to join a men's accountability group with him. He also corresponded with Dan a few times, sharing his weaknesses and asking for input. They also had a common bond. I get so excited when I think about how God takes care of even the littlest details of our lives when we surrender our all to Him.

JEANIE

Remember Jeanie, Lori's friend from church, and her struggle in her marriage with her husband's addiction to pornography and adultery? God also did a work of grace in her husband Tim's life and through a couple of different men challenging and encouraging him he walked away from his sin and they are back in church as a family, their marriage stronger than ever.

But during this time Jeanie also had some tragic events happen in her family. This is another area where the 1st Peter 3 girls shine. Prayer partners and encouragers.

Jeanie lost a young nephew in a drowning accident. She needed to be there for her sister. It devastated the family. But someone needed to be there for Jeanie. As most of us in the group are mothers, our hearts went out to her sister and the entire family as we shared Jeanie's grief. It was a stress on her marriage also as her sister lived out of town and she was trying to be there for her as well as still meet the needs of Tim and hold her own children close.

Her brother-in-law was also dealing with alcoholism, which only compounded the tragedy. Jeanie's sister and husband were not believers and through the process of grieving and healing, Jeanie was able to witness to her sister and within a few months she had accepted God's gift of grace. Huge answers to prayer. We are still praying for her brother-in-law, trusting God's timing.

Tim and Jeanie continue to work on their relationship, putting God first and making sure there is accountability in their marriage. It's never easy, but with God it's *always* worth it.

JULIA

Julia, Maggie's co-worker, would also struggle with the issue of work and having a family. She and Kent had three children and he wanted her to quit her job and stay home to care for them. It's not that she didn't want to but again, it's that security thing for women. Kent, being the godly man that he is, gently led her and we were *her* cheering section for a change. She did it, the hard thing. She quit and shortly after that they were blessed with their fourth child. Andrew was such a blessing at this time in their lives. But shortly after he was born the doctor was concerned that he may have a hearing loss. They ran test after test. Not being able to definitely determine what the damage was but the doctors feeling that there certainly was something wrong. Being only a new born, some tests would have to wait weeks or even months to determine what, if anything was wrong.

The 1st Peter 3 girls were on it. Or I should say, on their knees about it. Regardless of what God's outcome would be, we were there for each other, supporting Julia and Kent at a time when they needed us. I also know there were many family and friends praying for Andrew.

Then came the tests that would let them know the extent of the damage and low and behold, Andrew was fine. We don't know if God healed him out right or the tests just determined there was no problem, but we *do* know that God was in control and watching over Andrew and for whatever reason, God took us down that path together. Teaching each of us to trust Him more, even when it's our kids and we want so badly to fix it for them.

MANDY

Mandy, Maggie's other co-worker who had joined our little group, had some exciting times too. Shortly after she and Bill married he began to drink again and things began to deteriorate rapidly. God had to teach Mandy about the "shut up" concept and getting out of the way so He could deal with Bill. Steven and Maggie had tried to spend some time with them and encourage them as a couple but Bill was withdrawing. They would end up moving out of town and they did not have a computer so it was difficult to keep in touch with Mandy. We thought of her often and missed her lively personality in our group very much but we were also prayerfully concerned that things would end badly knowing what the situation had been when they left.

Maggie would attempt to contact Mandy many times but with little success. She was able to speak with her a couple of times during the next year but it would be brief and Mandy would just say things were fine.

Then a year later, Maggie would get a call from Mandy. She and Bill wanted to come to town just to visit and tell her what had been happening in their lives. They knew she would understand. Things had apparently gotten pretty bad and, at one point, Bill had moved out and was staying somewhere else. Then a friend asked them to a dramatic presentation at their church and they had gone. God had been dealing with Bill since his conversion but he did not want to give up control.

God used this dramatic program to get their attention and Bill went forward and brought Mandy with him. It was a change like Dan had experienced. They made Jesus Lord of their lives and were so excited they wanted to let Maggie and the girls know.

And it all had started two years before when Maggie went out of her comfort zone and shared with Mandy.

Isn't it awesome how God works in our lives through people who are willing to be obedient to His Word? Look at the blessings we would have all missed if Lori and Maggie would have said, "No, I'm settling for the easy way out".

God works in each of our lives at different times on different things. Things aren't always resolved when we think they should be. Our 1st Peter 3 group is still in the process of doing what God has called us to do and some of us are still in the midst of less than perfect situations.

STACY

Stacy, my friend growing up, spent over two years dealing with the pain and heartache of a daughter in rebellion from God and rejecting her family. We all continued to pray that God would do whatever it took to get her attention. As a mother this is one of the most frightening, difficult things to do, to put your child totally in the hands of God and let go, knowing they are making choices that could destroy their lives. It was a very difficult few years for Stacy and her husband as they learned how to love Jill unconditionally yet not compromise their own beliefs. I know that this is the most painful thing Stacy has ever experienced but I also know that she has never felt so close to the Lord and had such an intimate relationship with Him. She knows more about trusting the God who is able more now than at any other time in her life and after the darkness there also came a dawning for Stacy and her family.

Eventually they would learn that Jill had become pregnant out of wedlock. Jill made the decision to marry the father and during the course of her pregnancy began spending time with Stacy as God gently drew her back to Himself. Healing had begun. Jill is now happily married with two children and attending church with her husband. Her relationship with her mother has been restored and although she will bear the scars of her rebellion, God has once again shown his grace and forgiveness in the midst of our human failure and rebellion. Stacy is also living proof of what God's grace can do in the middle of impossible heartache.

RENEE & TRACI

Then there is Renee and Traci. Both women, as I write this, are still in unresolved marriage situations.

Renee, my neighbor, is still living with a husband not fully committed to Christ in his walk and living very selfishly which robs the whole family of a Godly husband and father. But more importantly, Brian is robbing himself of the blessings that await him, like Dan had been, when he finally chooses to take up the mantle God has chosen for him. Renee has had to deal with at least five times in the past few years when her husband questioned whether or not he loved her and wanted to stay married. Each time she has learned more about the love of God and trusting Him even when, like in both Maggie and Lori's cases, it looked more than impossible. We are still praying for Brian and regardless of his ultimate choices, know beyond a shadow of a doubt that God will bless Renee's faithfulness and commitment to Him.

Last but not least is Traci, my friend from Jr. High that God brought back into my life after many years. Traci has brought somewhat of a change to our group. Where as the other women are still married, even if not in the best of circumstances, Traci is still alone. Kyle left her over a year ago and after repeated attempts to encourage him to seek counseling together with her or even alone, Kyle filed divorce papers a few months ago.

We are dealing with an entirely different set of circumstances, yet still, humans are human and sin is still sin. Kyle, as I said in earlier chapters, does not have a personal relationship with Christ and wants absolutely nothing to do with God or church. As we try to encourage Traci with Biblical principles, we have tried to keep in front of us the reality that God is still in control and if she will continue to seek His face and submit to His Word, God will honor her obedience regardless of what Kyle does. Either way God *will* provide for Traci as long as she remains in His will *being* who God wants her to be.

The difficult part is waiting and at times, not knowing how to encourage or comfort in this particular kind of situation. Being married to a non-believer, the Bible is clear that Traci is free to let him go if he chooses to leave.

I Cor 7:15-16 "But if the unbeliever leaves, let him do so. A believing man or woman is not bound in such circumstances. God has called us to live in peace. How do you know, wife, if you will save your husband? Or how do you know, husband, if you will save your wife?" NIV

We believe that God can reach Traci's husband, but as verse 16 says, we don't know what Kyle's decision will be. We have to trust and leave it in God's hands and at this point, Kyle has chosen to walk away from his marriage and the divorce is to be final soon.

We are all learning together and it has been a good growing experience for us all. Yet in our humanity and doubts we still have to remind ourselves that God is ALWAYS big enough to do the impossible but only He knows what that ultimately is. So we wait. And pray. And try to encourage Traci in discerning how, according to God's Word, He would have her live and comport herself during the waiting. This has not been easy on any of us but as a group we are committed to God's purpose for bringing us together and committed to caring and loving one another through the most difficult times.

There have been many times over the years that we have not seen eye to eye, even on interpreting verses and Biblical principles and how we each have chosen to apply them in our lives. The great thing is that as we have learned to *practically* apply God's Word and support each other in doing so, we have matured in our relationships and learned more than just marriage principles or even what to do as wives. We have learned how to lovingly confront, communicate and forgive the way Jesus admonished in the New Testament.

To be perfectly honest, at times this has been very painful. As in any intimate relationship, there will be conflict at times and miscommunication. Early on, we set up boundaries and guidelines and asked that each woman honor these guidelines out of respect for the others in the group and to keep the commitment to God's Word the primary basis for our dialogue.

There are some key verses that we have used in situations that have arisen that have helped us in our growth together.

Prov 27:17 "As iron sharpens iron, so one man sharpens another." NIV

Prov 27:6a "Wounds from a friend can be trusted" NIV

Heb 10:24, 25b "Let us consider how we may spur one another on toward love and good deeds... ...but let us encourage one another, and all the more as you see the Day approaching." NIV

Luke 17:3-4 "So watch yourselves. If your brother sins, rebuke him, and if he repents, forgive him. If he sins against you seven times in a day and seven times comes back to you and says, 'I repent,' forgive him." NIV

James 5:16 and 19-20 "Therefore, confess your sins to each other and pray for each other so that you may be healed."

"My brothers (sisters), if one of you should wander from the Truth and someone should bring him back, remember this: Whoever turns a sinner from the error of his way will save him from death and cover over a multitude of sins." NIV

1st Peter 4:8 "Above all, love each other deeply, because love covers over a multitude of sins." NIV

Biblical foundation is critical in our own individual lives and in dealing with each other in the Body of Christ. Applying God's Word is the only way to make relationships really work and become fulfilling and intimate. And as we plug away in our humanness, working through so many different issues together, we have learned much about God's grace and forgiveness.

This brings me to the final member of the group to introduce you to and the most difficult chapter for me to write. So here goes...

CHAPTER EIGHTEEN

"You Ain't All That, Girlfriend!"

Of course, you know by now that my name is Marlene and if you've been paying attention you have picked up on that fact that I always have an opinion. Just ask me. But *don't* ask out of politeness or courtesy unless you want to hear it because I *will* give you an honest answer. I don't know if that is a blessing or a curse at times but it may be why I ended up being the unofficial leader of the 1st Peter 3 girls.

The most difficult thing for me to do is to tell you about who I am. It is far easier to tell you that I know Who put me here. But I struggle with the 'whys' because I still, at times, wrestle with God regarding my gifts and abilities.

I do not have a heart-wrenching, tragic story to tell about my marriage. I have been married for over 20 years to a wonderful, godly man. I have not been through much of the tremendous pain and disillusionment that most of these women have experienced. My two teenage children have personal relationships with Jesus Christ and at this point are committed to walking with Him and are growing and I am very proud of them. I had a wonderful childhood growing up as a pastor's daughter in a loving, Christian home and feel very blessed for having the parents that I had. Don't get me wrong, I was not, and am not, perfect. I have dealt with my own issues of adolescent rebellion and also struggled as an adult. But I came to know Jesus Christ at an early age and have never really had a time in my life where I turned away in total rebellion and felt the need to "sow my wild oats". I look at the struggles that I have had in my life, and yes there have been some, but they are nothing compared to what thousands of women face every day in our society, in our neighborhoods and in our churches.

So why am I here? How can I disciple or help anyone when I cannot personally relate to many of the situations that these women face?

"Lord, why me?" Then, that small, still voice said, "IT'S NOT ABOUT YOU, MARLENE!"

"Oh!"

How arrogant of me to question God who loved me enough to die for me. Who created me and knew me before the foundations of the earth. I AM a sinner. I am no different than any other person who was lost in sin, heading for hell, and miraculously saved by God's wonderful grace.

No matter where we come from and what our situations, we all stand before God unworthy without the forgiveness of His Son. God's Word applies to me just as it applies to anyone who believes in the eternal, almighty God and wants to follow Him. It isn't easy for anyone.

At times I think it is almost easier for someone who was raised knowing the right things to say and do to cover and hide the most insidious sins in our hearts. Following God is not just about "outwardly doing", it is more about "inwardly being" who God wants you to be and we *all* have to press on toward the goal. We never 'arrive'. Each of us is given spiritual gifts that God expects us to use and not to disqualify ourselves because we think we aren't good enough or maybe we think we're too good. Either way the attitude is sin.

It is our calling, Ladies, to glorify God, not ourselves. The focus is not me, it is God and His awesomeness. Yes I struggle, at times with God's call on my life, but if I do not respond to His call and use the gifts He graciously gave, then I fail to point others to Him and I end up being the focus, which again is sin.

Because of my background and my marriage situation, I have had many women say to me "You just don't understand. You don't live with my husband." Or "You've never had to live through a divorce." And they are right. I have never had to deal with some of these things but I *do* happen to know what God's Word says. *I know the God who understands and The Jesus who has suffered far worse for each of us than any of us will ever be able to comprehend.* A pastor does not have to have experienced everything each member of his congregation is going through to preach the Word and for God to use it. God knows and His Word works *no matter what the circumstances or who you're dealing with.* It goes back to "is God who he says He is and is the Bible true?"

My God does miracles in my life. They may not be spectacular to the world, but they are, none the less, miracles because I am human and sinful and need His grace everyday to be who He wants me to be, just like you. So lest you are reading this thinking that these are nice stories but that they have nothing to do with you or that the principles do not apply to you or your situation, THINK AGAIN SISTER!

I can say on the authority of *God's Word*, not mine, that it's time to shut up ladies, according to 1st Peter 3. It is something I deal with. It is something that every woman I've ever met, regardless of her circumstance, has had to deal with at one point or another because we are all human and struggle with our sin nature.

Don't ever look at someone and judge his or her life just by what you think you see. You may never know the pain or struggles someone is going through. Don't assume that someone has the perfect life and then tell yourself that you are of no value to them because you don't and you can't live up to someone else's standard. At the same time, do not assume that because you have *not* been through what someone else has, that you cannot minister to them or challenge them according to the Word. The standard for all of us is Christ and every one of us falls short on our best day, in our own strength, without the Holy Spirit to guide and empower us. We cannot use each other as excuses not to be who *God* wants us to be. And we cannot lie and pretend to have it all together, jumping through hoops and somehow become self-righteous, ineffective clones of someone else's idea of what a Christian's life ought to look like.

I struggle with the same attitudes and sins that everyone else does, that the 1st Peter 3 girls all do. As a woman, I struggle with submission and that quiet and gentle spirit thing. I need accountability and encouragement. I need the other parts of the Body of Christ to be effective in my spiritual waik and personal ministry.

I am humbled by the faith I find in these women, my sisters in Christ. I know what the truth is and I know I have to apply it in my own life, but to watch them claim the same truth in their circumstances leaves me in awe of how great my God truly is and it spurs me on to trust Him more.

I come from a long line of fire and brimstone preachers and it seems to me that God has quite a sense of humor to pass on a tendency to be preachy to a woman. Or would that be a result of the fall? In this day and age when the role of women in the church has been such a huge controversy in evangelical organizations, possessing a passion to share and speak the Truth can be misunderstood. You see? I wrestle with God over where He is taking me. I resist being considered the leader of this group, yet am compelled to press on and reach out to women as God continues to open door after door.

With every gift, because of the fall and the sin we struggle with, there seems to be a down side. Tendencies we have to allow sin and Satan to distort our spiritual gifts or to use them for our own glorification. This scares me to death. But God has not given us a spirit of fear. He expects me to obey His direction in my life. In His infinite wisdom He has given me these wonderful women to hold me accountable to His Word to use what God has given me, not abuse it.

Maggie loves to remind me that "you ain't all that girlfriend". I can't afford to take myself too seriously. None of us can. We are all in the same boat. Sinners saved by grace, each with God given gifts and abilities to press on *together* for the prize of the high calling in Christ Jesus.

We have each, including myself, faced defining moments in our lives. Moments where God has gotten our attention and asked us to submit to His will. Moments that, having faced them, give us common ground to relate to one another on, that challenged us as individuals and grew us as children of God.

So who is Marlene? I'm just an average, normal (some would argue with that) wife and mother of two who wants to be who God wants me to be. I want women to know this God that I know. The God who loves them and wants to heal their hurts and turn their mundane lives into a great spiritual adventure. To know the God who wants to bless their relationships with a maturity and intimacy that they can never know without Him. I want them to know the passion I feel for God and for them and I want nothing more than for them to get a glimpse of Him and His power through His Word. To know, that no matter what, that God cares and still does do miracles. And regardless of whether or not you are facing tremendous difficulty at this time in your life, or whether you have been blessed with a Godly, working, intimate marriage, you have value to God and to the other women in your life.

I have a place here, but so do others. I need these women and their spiritual encouragement, guidance and insight in my life. And they need me. As Christians we have a responsibility to one another according to God's Word, whether it be to pray, encourage, exhort, teach or even discipline we must be committed to each other even in our inadequacies. We need each other as women in the Body of Christ.

God has used several women in my life over the years to challenge and mentor me, long before God gave me the 1st Peter 3 girls. I was blessed with a godly mother who was a living example of loving submission and discipline. Then, as a young wife, God brought Sherry into my life, who began as my ministry supervisor at Youth For Christ, but she has become so much more over the years. She has been, and still is, a great source of encouragement and a godly example to me, challenging me in my walk with Christ, in my marriage and as a mother. The Lord continues to bless me with godly women who impact my life. My pastor's wife, Sharon, has been a source of great encouragement and another friend involved in full time ministry, Diane, has challenged and encouraged me personally and in ministry. These women and others, God has given to enrich my life and sharpen me in His Word. These women were willing to get involved and invest themselves in me and I have learned much from them and their walk with the Lord. I, in turn, am challenged to do the same for others.

Titus 2:3-4 "... Teach the older women...then they can train the younger women to love their husbands and children..." NIV

As you read this, are there women in your life that come to mind, that you have allowed to teach you and instruct you and come along side you to encourage you in your journey as a godly woman? Are you involved in the lives of your sisters, investing in their growth and sharing your gifts knowledge and experiences?

We are all called to teach and to learn from each other as women. Which brings me to the next chapter. There are a few things God that has been working on and teaching me in my life over the past few years that

I'd like to share with you. So, as we say in the 1st Peter 3 group, here's my two cents…

CHAPTER NINETEEN

"My Two Cents…"

There are a couple of issues we have dealt with individually and collectively in the 1st Peter 3 group that I want to share with you so please bear with me while I get "preachy".

THE "S" WORD

One of the most difficult issues for us to tackle as women seems to be the "S" word in marriage. And no it's not "sex" although, as I mentioned earlier, we have dealt with that one too.

The "S" word that seems to cause the most problems for women would be *submission*. Just saying the word makes most women's skin crawl. It conjures up visions of being dragged around by the hair by some Neanderthal husband. Our present day society has so distorted the meaning of the word 'submission' that we don't even like to say the word, much less address the Biblical instruction regarding it. We are so afraid of it we seem to just skim over it as if it isn't really relative any longer. This would be another lie from Satan that robs us of God's blessing.

I would like to propose a different view of the dreaded concept. What I believe to be a Biblical perspective. That submission is a *pro-active action*, not just a passive response to negative or dictatorial authority. What submission is *not* is something to be *enforced* by husbands. It is to be our *willing* response to *God* and *His* will for our lives. It is not to be a doormat or to be controlled by another. It is an act of my will toward *God.* It is to be controlled by the Holy Spirit.

For most women submission does not come naturally. On our best day we struggle with our sinful nature. But because we have allowed ourselves to be convinced by society and the women's liberation movement in this country in the last three decades that we must rebel against any male authority, we have settled for carnal, superficial relationships at best. Or at worst we have turned our marriages into war zones that end in the carnage of divorce where no one wins.

It is, at times, subtle in its' attack on our spiritual lives. Several years ago the Lord dealt with me on an area of my life where I wasn't submitting to my husband's authority in my marriage. It happened just shortly before I was to speak at a women's retreat in Pennsylvania.

For about eight years my husband, Len, had been working 2nd shift at his job. This had worked well for us while the kids were little and not in school. He was home the better part of the day with us and then when the kids went to bed early I would have a few hours to myself to regroup and relax. As they got older and in school, it became more and more difficult to juggle our schedules with work and the kids and still make our marriage relationship a priority.

I have always been a little spoiled and naturally tend to be selfish and undisciplined and I had gotten into a comfortable routine in the evenings of enjoying "my time". I am a night person, definitely NOT a morning person, so I enjoyed staying up, telling myself

I was waiting for Len to be up when he got home. I was fooling myself. My time was about ME. I got hooked on several television shows, which I did not like to miss. The medical drama ER being one of them at the time. Of course the shows I enjoyed would come on at 10:00pm which is when Len got off work. He would walk in the door about 10:30 and by then I was engrossed in some dramatic episode and would distractedly greet him, barely giving him the time of day. He would want to unwind and spend some time together but I would always say, "just wait until this is over". By the time the show was over I would want to catch the news and by the end of that Len was falling asleep, exhausted and we hadn't connected at all. I had even gotten to where I moved an old black and white portable TV set in our bedroom.

This went on for some time until Len finally said something. He wanted the TV out of our bedroom. WHY? This wasn't fair. He was gone all evening and I was all alone, with the kids in bed. I needed to unwind and relax. He wasn't even there so why did it matter?

He said he felt like I didn't want to spend any time with him. That I put my shows before him and he was just an after thought. Of course I argued. I can be oh so eloquent. I had my reasons. He was being unreasonable. Of course I cared and I did spend time with him. On and on the struggle went. I would move the TV out of the room and then a couple weeks later would get lazy and move it back.

We argued. Len became more and more frustrated. He even threatened to throw it out the window. "Oh, *that's* mature." I'd taunt. It is amazing to me that I could be so ridiculous and selfish. The more we argued the more committed to getting my way I was.

And then it stopped. Len quit talking. He didn't say anything for months about it. I felt justified. I wasn't doing anything *wrong*. Right? Just not submitting is all. Just not respecting my husband's authority. Just putting myself before my husband. Just robbing myself of a more intimate relationship with the man I said I loved.

Len was hurt and worried. He felt this issue had come between us but he no longer yelled or shared his feelings about it. I remember bringing it up at one point and he simply said, "You know how I feel" and left it at that.

I began to have this nagging feeling that I was perhaps *wrong.* An amazing thought. But I pushed it away. Ignored it.

Then my amazing, godly husband took control. In his gentle, servant leadership he took action in a way that totally broke and melted my heart.

I had come home on this particular day in the evening. I had gotten the kids in bed and hadn't even been to my room yet. It was dark and I couldn't see well but I headed for, you guessed it, the TV. I would just turn it on and then get ready for bed. As I reached the television I noticed a large piece of paper taped to the screen and the on button wasn't working. It must be unplugged. Curious, I grabbed the paper and went to turn the light on to read what it said.

As the light came on I was shocked at what I saw. Not only was the TV unplugged but an 18inch spike screwdriver had been driven through the top and into the picture tube. Breathless I read this note:

> *"I Len Lawson, protector and guide of this home, have given*
> *every effort to negotiate with this enemy, to keep himself from*
> *this room without success. Therefore I have slain this vampire*
> *with a stake through the heart. He shall no longer suck the*
> *life giving blood from this relationship.*
> *In Humble Service to My Queen"*

I sat down on my bed and wept. I knew I had been wrong. And I knew Len had not done this out of anger. He was totally in control when he took action as the head of our marriage to stop the deterioration of our relationship.

You see we all deal with issues in our lives and we all are to keep pressing on toward the goal of Christ's high calling, not mine or yours.

We have lost our focus and do not understand what a privilege it is to be a godly woman and to even find joy and purpose in the responsibility of submission in marriage. Because we have once again bought the lie, if and when we do subject ourselves to our husband's authority, it is with negative, resentful attitudes which will in fact undermine and destroy the very thing we as women want most in our husbands and marriages, unconditional love and security. As I have said before, we emasculate our husbands on a daily basis by our attitudes and with our tongues and then wonder why they don't show us the love and tenderness we crave.

But remember, this in not about manipulation. Submission is not something we do to get what we want. It is about our relationship with Christ first. He was there when we were formed in our mother's womb. He knows us best and knows what He created us for.

1 Peter 3 does not guarantee that *if* you submit then your husband will do what you want or be the man *you* think he ought to be. I believe God's Word teaches that when you submit with a Godly attitude you cease being a stumbling block in your husbands' life and then your witness can be used by God to reach him for *God*, not for your own purpose or pleasure. It is to honor God in your life and your husbands'. And remember we cannot control or make another person choose to follow God. It is that person's choice and you have no guarantee they will do what God asks. Just as you have a choice, so does your husband. I would much rather someone be honest with me and then wait on God's direction than try to force or manipulate a response that does not come from the heart because it will not last and it is not real.

Do not be deceived in thinking that submission is a negative, undesirable drudgery nor is it a manipulative ploy. It is a pro-active role that God gives us the privilege of fulfilling with His power. Do not also be deceived into thinking that the quiet and gentle spirit that 1st Peter 3 talks about is somehow simply an outward behavior. It is not about personality because God is a God of diversity and we each have different colorful personality traits. Some of the most controlling, unsubmissive women I have ever known are very meek and quiet in their outward behavior but very manipulative and deceptive in their relationships with their husbands. Treating their husbands as objects to be controlled through their behavior, seeming to outwardly reverence their husbands but in reality having no respect for their leadership.

Be confident in your role. Let your quiet and gentle spirit come from within, from a calm confidence and quiet grace that comes from knowing Who is ultimately in control and that you can trust Him implicitly.

So how does submission and "shutting up" fit together?

Let's take another look at 1st Peter 3.

HELP! I'M TALKING AND I CAN'T SHUT UP!

Ever felt like you just can't stop talking? That if you just *say* it enough or the right way he'll get it? It'll finally make sense? Don't worry you're not alone. I think it's a gender hazard.

One of the missions of our group is to help each other recognize our patterns of going on and on when we need to shut up. It is such a common problem that it has become a standing joke. Lori, at one point, wrote on email, "HELP! I'm talking and I can't shut up!"

We all laugh because we can TOTALLY relate! She recognized that she was talking herself to death and the only one getting more and more frustrated was *LORI!* Dan didn't seem to be "getting it" and she was becoming more and more miserable. She was also getting in between God and Dan and what He was doing with Dan. Instead of being confronted by God, all Dan saw was Lori's *nagging.* She came off as critical, negative and even self-righteous at times. Was this her intent? No. She just wanted Dan to understand.

"But, don't you see…?" "How can you *not* understand what I'm saying…?

We've all been there, done that one. Then we come to the group frustrated and venting.

"Why can't he see it? What if he never does…? Why… What if…?

SHUT UP GIRLFRIEND! Be wallpaper; pleasant but in the background. Pop that corn and sit back and watch God work. Get your eyes off your husband and onto God. What is God teaching *you* regardless of what your husband does?

Do not become the foolish woman who tears down her own house. Do not become a stumbling block, lying down in front of your husband, tripping him. You will cause him to fall and when he does, he will fall right on top of you and you will both suffer.

Get out of the way and just shut up! This applies to all of us, regardless of where your marriage is. Because we are all human, even the best of marriages go through difficult times and as Christians we get lazy. When we begin to take God for granted, the results begin to show up in all areas of our lives including, or I should say *especially* our marriages.

It is very difficult to submit to God and consequently to our husbands as head of the home when we do not exercise the discipline of knowing when to keep quiet. When all we are doing is talking because we think that we know best what God wants our husbands to be then we miss hearing the still small voice of God in our own lives. Again, it's the "go wait in the waiting room and let the master mechanic work" principle.

We tend to talk ourselves right out of the very thing we say we want. We must not settle for less than God's best for ourselves *or* our husbands. Do not let your desire for your husband be motivated by selfish motives. Do not think that if he would do what you wanted or be who you think he should that that would be the best for him or you. The best is *God's* best that we should seek and we cannot see what that is at times until we have gone through the worst of times and come through on the other side *changed*, not just different circumstances. We need to check our motives when we think we need to talk, or when we do shut up, or even when we submit. I cannot stress enough that this is *not* about manipulation. It is about *you* being who God wants *you* to be. I have said many times that when God changes you it does not change your husband but it changes the equation and therefore the outcome. $2 + 2 = 4$ until you change one of the factors. It does not change the other factor but it *does* change the end product. Your husband may not change, that is between him and God, but it will change the dynamics of the relationship and the Lord will bless your obedience. Your husband has a choice just as you do and God is big enough to deal with him, you worry about YOU.

Our pastor has always said when talking to couples that it is far better to be second in someone's life who has put God first than to be first in someone's life without God. It can be very scary to let go and trust God but that *is* what it is about, trusting God.

Maggie has often said that if she had gotten what she thought she wanted when she wanted it through all of this she would not have ever changed. She would still be controlled by the sin of her anger and bitterness and would not have learned how to be who God wants her to be. She would have missed the blessing, not to mention she would certainly be divorced.

Ultimately, in a growing, thriving marriage based upon Biblical principles there *is* two way communication. There is sharing and intimacy. But 1st Peter 3 specifically addresses *"...if any of them (husbands) do **not** believe the Word, they may be won over **without talk** by the behavior of their wives..." 1st Peter 3:1 NIV.* I am not saying we are never to communicate with our husbands, but the Bible gives clear direction in our lives of how to be pro-active and Godly wives regardless of what our husbands choose.

The best thing you can do for your husband, whether he is walking with the Lord or choosing not to is PRAY, PRAY, PRAY for him.

And while you're at it, pray for God to show you where you need to be. Know your role, come up with a plan on how you need to fill that role, and be confident and content in the place God has called you to be. I also believe that if just one person in the relationship will let God get a hold of them and they will submit themselves to His will, husband *or* wife, miracles will happen in the individuals life and then even the marriage. And they have.

CHAPTER TWENTY

"One More Thing..."

Ok, the girls are laughing now. They know me too well. My two cents usually turns into a dollar and then some. But there is one more thing I would like to share regarding the issue of our Biblical roles in marriage.

THE TANDEM CONCEPT

For twenty years my husband Len has been trying to get me to get interested in biking. I am not a physically active person. I tell people that sweating is against my religion. He has mentioned over the years that he thought that maybe a tandem bike would be fun for the two of us. Something we could do together. A bicycle built for two. How romantic. It's a great idea, but we never got around to it.

Until recently, that is. Len and I went away for the weekend alone together to stay at a bed and breakfast near Lake Michigan. The kids were gone to a youth convention and we have always made getting away alone together a priority and this was a great chance. Len likes to plan the romantic get-aways a lot of the time so he went ahead and made the arrangements.

Earlier in the week he had asked me if I would still be interested in going biking on a tandem with him and I cautiously said "yes". He was up to something. The bed and breakfast was nice, and guess what they had? A bicycle built for two to use all we wanted. What a coincidence. He had seen in their advertisement that they had bicycles for use and had specifically asked for a tandem.

Being reluctant to "sweat" I was a little apprehensive about my ability to actually do this for any amount of time without having a coronary. But I was in for a pleasant surprise. It was a gorgeous sunny day with a cool breeze blowing in off the lake. Once we got started, five minutes did not go by and I had a revelation. This was a *spiritual* concept. The bicycle built for two was a perfect picture of marriage. Well, maybe not perfect but definitely a great object lesson.

I, of course, had to share it with Len. All afternoon. Everything we did and everywhere we went I could see the spiritual application in marriage. He had taken the front seat. His role was to lead. Even though we both were peddling, he determined what direction we would take. He would caution me if there was a bump or if we were turning. He told me when to lighten up on the peddling and when to coast. I, on the other hand, kept balance and peddled and helped with speed and momentum. I also had a great time just looking around. I so enjoyed the day I never even considered stopping. For three hours we biked. We went to the beach and enjoyed the view.

Then we had to tackle an ominous hill. Len asked me if I wanted to get off and walk the bike up together or go back another way. I said, "No, we can do it". Half way up I thought I was going to die but kept saying, "we can do this".

At the top of the hill we stopped to enjoy the view. It was breathtaking and we enjoyed the feeling of accomplishment together. Just past the crest of the hill were two benches overlooking the lake in a quaint neighborhood near an old church and had we not attempted the hill we would have missed the cozy, intimate spot.

All day long I kept thinking, 'this is what God intended'. Such a simple thing but such a profound truth. If I had not worked with Len, if I had wanted to control the bike myself, if I had not peddled with him up that hill and refused to go, not only would we have missed so much beauty, we would have more than likely fallen and wrecked the bike. We would have been frustrated with each other and there was the definite possibility we would have gotten hurt. Each trying to do the others job but not being in the right position on the bike would have been disastrous.

I don't know about you but every time we go somewhere we forget something. Well, I had forgotten a camera. I was so impressed with the beauty of the day and the spiritual parallels I could see in what we were doing that I suggested we bike to a store to buy a disposable camera. The store was a considerable distance from the Lake and then I wanted to bike back down to the beach, take that same hill again and take pictures at every step so I wouldn't forget.

That is the commitment God expects us to have to Him and to our marriages and the men we promised to love honor and obey. In sickness and in health, for richer or poorer, till death do us part.

It was so important to work together. To make choices about which position each of us needed to take, and whose job was what, and then how to carry out the responsibilities of that position. This is how God asks us to work together in marriage. He has given us the blue print and assigned the roles to the best possible person for that role and in obeying Him, He expects and plans for us to actually enjoy the ride even when the work is hard. It is simply an attitude of obedience to God, accept your role in marriage, it is what you are called and equipped to do as a woman. If you have made the choice to be married then make the choice to be a godly wife. God won't let you down even when your husband does.

What an awesome lesson and what an awesome God that He can teach us even through our recreation and play times in life. It was a weekend I definitely will never forget and I have been after Len ever since to find us a tandem bike of our own.

I might even consider sweating.

CHAPTER TWENTY ONE

The Ultimate Make-Over

God has truly blessed this group of women as you have read but I have a fear as I write this to you. My fear is that women will read it and, as one song says, be "stirred but not changed". That this will somehow just be a nice story with a couple of happy endings. That is *not* what this is about. And just as this is not a "feel good" book the 1st Peter 3 girls are not just another "support group" or chat room. This is about *real* women who serve a *real* God who *changes lives.*

In our present culture we as women are bombarded with mixed messages from society and even the church. It is, as I have said earlier, that we have bought into the lie that says a woman's role is to compete, to succeed at all costs, and to conquer. We have been duped into giving up our gender distinctions and roles. As a result Christian women are trying to straddle the fence between secular society and Biblical principle and women in secular society are driving themselves into the ground chasing the brass ring they've been told is out there if they just "do it all". The results are spiritually shallow women who are not ever satisfied with their lives or themselves.

The role models the media has given us in the last few decades range from obnoxious Roseanne Barr to sophisticated and sexy Cindy Crawford, to buff and politically active Jane Fonda, to "spiritual" and spunky Shirley Mclain. Between the emphasis on physical perfection, professional success and the spiritual journey to find the "goddess inside", we don't know whether to work out, get a Ph.D., or just channel the aerobics instructor we used to be in a past life.

Women seem to be searching, as never before, for that illusive purpose and peace that brings meaning to life. At the retreat I was headed to when God dealt with me on that particular submission issue, the focus of my message for the weekend was "The Ultimate Makeover". I drew some simple parallels between our physical and spiritual lives as women.

Most women I know go through the "make-over frenzy" periodically. You know what that is. You feel hormonal, emotionally drained, too fat, too skinny, bored with your clothes, bored with your hair, dissatisfied with your life, you need a change. You go shopping and buy new make-up or clothes then call the hairdresser and get a haircut or perm or a color. You join the gym or take up a self-improvement class. Or you decide to go back to school for that degree you never finished. Just *something* to change that stagnate feeling. The feeling that your life isn't going anywhere and that it isn't valuable because you aren't "superwoman" yet.

As I mentioned earlier in the book, most women who use cosmetics understand the concept of applying make up. We usually have a goal, or picture in our minds of what we want the end results to be. Society has given us books, magazines, and various kinds of "media" manuals that instruct us as to what they think the modern woman should look like. The preferred careers, the trendy clothes, the correct products to buy and how to use them and the choices they tells us we have a "right" to make.

I would like to suggest that we put away all the secular manuals and go to the original, definitive book on makeovers and being successful women. The Bible.

God had the original blue print and it is still the best. Maybe you have been reading this and do not understand the relationship the women you have met in these pages have with Jesus Christ. You know *of* Him but do not know Him. Perhaps this parallel will help you understand what they have experienced and will challenge you to look at the ultimate beauty manual.

At the retreat I talked about the three steps in a good makeover: foundation, make-up, and finishing touches. I just want to share with you the principle of *foundation* because it is the most critical in the makeover process. The physical process first requires cleansing and treating blemishes before the foundation can be applied correctly. The obvious spiritual application here is, according to the Bible we all have unsightly dirt and blemishes on our souls, sin, and we have nothing on our own to clean and treat them with.

"For all have sinned and fall short of the Glory of God." Romans 3:23 NIV

God has the ultimate cleanser that does not just clean the surface but deep within the soul.

Remember application is everything so how do we apply that cleanser? By looking in God's mirror and seeing and then admitting that we actually have blemishes and dirt and then taking the cleanser from God that only He provides and allowing Him to clean our lives. Again, that ultimate cleanser being the sacrifice of God's Son Jesus on the cross, whose blood takes away the sin of the world. (*Rom 5:6-8*) But we have to accept His cleansing, knowing that we cannot do it ourselves.

"For it is by grace you have been saved, through faith – and this not from yourselves, it is the gift of God – not by works, so that no one can boast." Eph 2:8,9 NIV

God's foundation does not just cover our blemishes but takes them away and we then stand healed and unblemished before God. This foundation cannot be found at expensive cosmetic counters or exclusive beauty shops. It is priceless but He gives it freely to anyone who will come to the great beautician. That is the final step, application, and it is critical.

At expensive department stores many times they will offer free gifts with purchases of their cosmetics. A pretty bag or additional make-up with the purchase. With God there is no purchase to be made, it has already been paid for and the free bonus is eternal life for anyone who believes.

"That if you confess with your mouth, Jesus is Lord, and believe in your heart that God raised him from the dead; you will be saved, for it is with your heart that you believe and are justified, and it is with your mouth that you confess and are saved." Romans 10:9,10 NIV

"For everyone who calls on the name of the Lord will be saved." Romans 10:13 NIV

Our spiritual foundation becomes Christ and with God the foundation is universal. It works for everyone regardless of blemishes or color or background or baggage and it doesn't just cover, it totally removes them.

Then having applied the foundation, God moves on to adding the next steps in the makeover of our lives. Make-up and finishing touches. God uses His Holy Spirit to teach us character that adds color and definition to our lives and then he uses our own God given gifts, talents and abilities to round off a complete new creation. The finishing touches in a fulfilled, complete, successful life as a woman of God.

I hope you are challenged to read God's Word and look for those steps in your personal life. For those who have not recognized the value of applying spiritual foundation, I pray that you will see it in what you have read and go to the Ultimate Beautician for the makeover that will last for eternity. And for those of you who have accepted God's gift of salvation, I pray that you are challenged to look in God's Word for the make-up and finishing touches He wants to develop in your lives.

The 1st Peter 3 girls are committed to helping each other in the Ultimate Makeover process by holding up the mirror of God's Word. In the next chapter you will read in their own words how God has used this in each of their lives to develop lasting inner beauty that transcends the physical and is not diminished by circumstance.

CHAPTER TWENTY TWO

In Their Own Words

I have introduced you to these extraordinary women I call my sisters, and told their stories from my own vantage point in our relationships, but they have their own unique perspectives and circumstances that brought them to The 1st Peter 3 Girls. In the remainder of this chapter, several of the girls, along with Dan, share some of their own thoughts and some personal background with you that will fill in some of the gaps and, in their own words, tell what God has miraculously done in their lives.

RENEE

There is a country song called "Looking for Love in All the Wrong Places" and for the longest time, that was a way of life for me. Wallowing so deeply in unrealized self-pity, I roamed aimlessly looking for "just the right love". My philosophy being: if someone loves you enough they will do whatever it takes to please you. Now don't misunderstand me, this was not as selfish as it sounds. I lived what I expected. I gave, and gave until I was all used up and when that still wasn't enough I begged "What more can I do?" "What do you want me to be?"

I asked to be told my "shortcomings" and, by golly, was told them. Then how true they were became the issue. I had the right to defend myself! And in doing so I would respond by listing my husband's shortcomings. I think you can see where this was going…downhill fast!

This was a pattern in my life that repeated itself time and time again and in the end I was always left hurt, angry and blaming *him*. Where was I to turn? The man who was supposed to be my knight, my protector, my comfort and security was the one causing me all of my grief. Or was he?

When I met Marlene I knew I had met a truly special friend. She invited me to her church, and included me in her circle of friends. She reintroduced me to the Father who I thought hid behind a newspaper until it was time to pass judgment. And the Son who I thought could never repay *my* sins by dying for me, and so was therefore avoiding my "indebtedness". And to the Holy Spirit to whom my favorite saying was "la, la, la, I cant hear you" because I misunderstood His purpose.

Learning the Truth has changed my mind, my life, my heart, and, above all, my marriage. Don't get me wrong, it hasn't changed my husband. But it has changed how I view him and respond to him. It was difficult to stop passing judgement on him and turn the focus back to me, but the benefits far outweigh the burden. When there is a conflict I need to ask myself if I've done something to cause it. If so, I need to make the proper corrections and take responsibility for my own actions. If not, *let it go.* It is not mine to own. This is where faith in the fact that God is in control really shines through. You *can* be at peace in the middle of conflict if you just stay faithful to God's direction and purpose in your life.

I finally found that "true love" I had so longed for. I found Him in my Lord God. He and only He can be all of what I need in my life. God is totally true to His Word and the only way to really know this is by reading and learning His Word and then walking in His light through Jesus. Remember, if you put all of your faith in people, no matter how close or wonderful they are, at some point they *will* disappoint you. I have learned to put my faith in God and encourage anyone to give your heart to Him because He will never let you down.

As we all, at times, trip and fall along the path to God's Glory, we as 1st Peter 3 girls have made the commitment to be the helping hands to lift each other back up. As we encourage each other, we remind ourselves as well. Too often we judge others by our own negative experiences or regrets due to poor choices made in our past that have left us cold and bitter, denying the chance for joy. God views our struggles as learning experiences to be grateful for. Without lessons there is no learning, and without learning there is no growth.

Because we do tend to stray, God puts up guardrails. The effect of contact with them is directly proportional to the velocity at which we hit the rail! We can also catch a case of whiplash due to someone else's driving (which is often the case, I've found, in marriage). This still is an opportunity for learning and growth. Angry, hurtful responses never seem to produce positive results. However, as humans we do get angry and hurt and we react. We fall short of God's righteousness. Thus, the need for accountability. Our 1st Peter 3 group developed from just such a need.

Christian women, dedicated but human, sharing and supporting with "in your face" Gospel, holding each other accountable, yet loving and forgiving. The group has become a lifeline for me. Not only do we help each other stay on track in our roles as wives and our Christian walk, but we learn to reach out to others by sharing, even each others' experiences that we may not have experienced ourselves. Though we all have different perspectives, we have one common core – our Lord Jesus Christ.

It is truly a blessing to be born again and have a group of women who care enough to never let me go back to the person I first saw looking in "God's mirror". The power of prayer is unstoppable! Do so often, it works for us!

ERICA

This group has meant so much to me. At first it was just great to have contact with other women out there. Being far from family and old friends, I had felt so "on-my-own" at mothering, being a wife, and just plain living. So the group provided feedback, answers, and suggestions on these things. But now, after time, the group has come to mean a whole lot more than that to me. The 1 Peter 3 group is spiritual support, in a real, honest, caring way.

We challenge each other to pray without ceasing, we pray for each other and all the situations that come up. The group has also given me spiritual perspective I need. We throw out our opinions and challenge each other on what scripture means and how it applies to us today as wives and moms.

And then there's the accountability. I became very grateful for this after something my husband and I dealt with, and still are. I emailed the group about a "possible" problem I thought my husband might have with pornography. I was almost light hearted about explaining my concern and figured I didn't have much to worry about. I figured the group would think I was just overreacting. And I thought I just needed to believe him when he said there was "no problem". Then came the "get-real-face-it-then-watch-God-move" words from the group. I got a phone call from one of the girls, and I later realized how much I needed that wake-up call. As result of the encouraging but challenging words from the group I was able to see the problem for what it was and how I should handle myself and respond to my husband. To make a long story short, my husband and I dealt with the problem face to face, and after the yelling, crying and honesty, we gave it all to God and my husband was then free. The problem isn't just gone but it's now being fought with God in control and not hidden away anymore.

I am so glad that God brought me into this group. He definitely knew I needed them. I have grown and stretched and mostly have gotten real about what's important in my marriage based on what the Bible and God wants for us. I believe, as Christians, we all need this type of thing with other women. We need to be there for each other. Oh, and one more thing, we have a whole lot of fun along the way!

JEANIE

"What God has put together, let not man separate."

This was our unspoken rule. We were both Christians when we married. Tim had been the one who had led me to Christ a few years before our marriage. We had sought counsel from our pastors. We knew we were right for each other. We loved each other.

Each of our parents had divorced. My father was an alcoholic, had committed adultery and had remarried. Tim's father had also committed adultery and remarried. We were aware it happened, but "it" never would to us. It was not an option. "It" being adultery and divorce. Because of our "rule" I really didn't let the thought that we would have serious problems enter my mind. I lived in a fantasy world.

We had been married six years. We had two small children. We lived in a new city. Tim and I both had new jobs. We lived in our first home. I was busy with involvement with ministries at church and Tim spent a lot of time at the computer. With two small children at our feet we had little time or energy for one another but I thought that was normal.

My journal entry for the fall of that year read: "Lord, please give me strength to get through these tough times…help me to <u>choose</u> to love my husband, …What is going on with Tim…please change me Lord."

I remember that our Sunday school lessons were very good. We were doing the Homebuilder's Study. I was learning a lot. It was in Sunday school that I heard Maggie's story and how God was working in their marriage. God's timing *is* perfect. The "wake-up call" came the following January. I discovered Tim was involved in pornography. I then got a clearer picture of what was happening to our marriage. But I was in shock.

Looking back, I know that God only allowed me to learn part of the problem, because that was all that I could handle at that time. God will not give me anything more than I can handle!

Tim apologized and said he would do some things and I believed that everything would be fine. I dove into the Bible for strength. It was then that I began searching for answers to the many questions I had. Why? How could *this* happen to us? Our "perfect" marriage was ruined, I thought. It could never be the same ever again.

In May of that year, I met Maggie who, along with Marlene, was sharing her testimony at a local women's Promise Reapers Seminar. As I sat and listened to her speak about what she had been through, I had hope that I, also, could get through this.

By August I could tell that things were not going very well with Tim. He was very withdrawn, distant and did not want to talk about plans in our future. Then in October I discovered the reason for his behavior. Tim was out of town with his job and I had three days to search our home. What I found shocked me enough to reach out for help. I called Lori. I had known that she was also having marriage problems. She talked and prayed with me and encouraged me to call Marlene. I spent the next few days in prayer and fasting and searching the Bible for help. Until this time I had never felt the loving hands of God holding me. Inside I wanted to die. But I knew I couldn't. I had called a few friends for prayer and I truly felt bathed in prayer.

I know that it was by God's strength alone that I got through those few days and by His peace that I was able to confront Tim when he returned home. I confronted him in calmness, yet firmly with boundaries set. Then I left for the night to give him some time to make his decision to either choose sin or his family. As I drove, about an hour's distance away to the home of the Pastor who had married us, I could feel God's presence as He directed our van down the highway. The children were screaming for their daddy and I was second-guessing if I was doing the right thing. Since Tim had just told me that he no longer loved me, nor liked being married, I was uncertain of what the future held for my family. But I knew that we could not continue to live with the sin. God wanted much better for us.

That entire night I prayed and cried. God comforted me. I yearned to read His promises. I had never *needed* God so much, and he was there. Holding me.

The next day Tim called and asked us to come home. He said that he couldn't promise anything and that it would never be the same, but he still wanted us to come. At first I wanted to go back to our "old marriage" and then I realized that it could *never* be the same. And I was glad. I didn't want the lies and secrecy. He had become a stranger to me. We both wanted it different. It was very hard. I had to learn that *I* needed to change, not just Tim. We attended a Family Life Marriage Seminar and I heard the speaker say, "Maybe God is so busy trying to work on changing you that He cant even begin to work on your husband." He was saying that to *me*. Wow! That hit hard. I began to realize that I had problems, too. A marriage takes two to make and two to break. Tim's addictions were his own, but I also had problems. I had to deal with control issues. I had to give these over to God and step aside and not be so co-dependant on Tim.

There were times when I was repulsed to be in the same bed with my husband. It was when I would think about all that had happened and how differently our marriage was turning out that it was so difficult to handle. But God showed me that I had made my marriage vows not only to Tim, but also to God. I also was responsible for my own actions toward my husband. I knew that one day I would stand before our King and give my account of my behavior regardless of what he had done.

It was about this time that I joined the 1st Peter 3 girls. I had been talking to Lori and Marlene but I hadn't joined the rest on Email until this point. Maggie would share word pictures that helped me visualize how I needed to react toward my husband. The group encouraged me in prayer and in words. They reminded me, "Two steps forward, one step back." "One day at a time, but always moving forward." "God is in control and still working." "God is big enough, whatever it takes."

The following spring, in May, my five-year-old nephew was killed suddenly in an accident. The same age as our oldest child. It was a very difficult time for our families. I spent a lot of time with my sister. I think it really made Tim see how precious our lives are. How quickly things can change. The following July Tim attended church for the first time in 9 months. He would come for special programs the children were in but it would be another year before I really felt the change.

But in the meantime God was still working on me. Lori had shared with the group her struggle with another man who had been calling her and asked for accountability. We talked about being guardrails for each other. I also was vulnerable because of my marriage situation and was feeling unloved and not needed. Lonely. I felt myself slipping into a similar situation as Lori's. Because she had shared with the group, I was alert to what was happening and quickly ended all contact with a man I had been friends with. God taught me that I wasn't beyond sin and that what I was doing was sin in God's eyes just as much as what Tim had done. I was still learning.

In May of our 9th year of marriage, 3 years after my journal entry, Tim and I had another heated discussion. The turning point came when he said, "You don't know and may never trust me again, but *I do – I know I'm right before God.*"

It was like my heart stopped. That was the first time in our marriage that I heard and saw Tim take the lead. I knew I had to step back. I did so with joy and relief that Tim was finally right with God.

Looking back I know that God was teaching me to trust him more. Not only with myself but also with my husband and my family. I know that if I had learned everything that had been going on that first night 3 years before, I would not have handled myself according to God's will. Tim has said that if I had handled it any differently emotionally, or by threatening, he would have probably left. He said that he went back and forth a hundred times whether to leave or stay. He didn't promise anything but it would have to be a miracle.

God still does miracles! We are soon going to be celebrating our 10th year of marriage. it has never been so good! I have never loved him more. God has shown us the blessing by obeying Him. When I sought advice, many people, even some Christians, said that it would be "understandable" for me to divorce Tim. After all, he had committed such great sins and I could just wash him away from my life.

If I had taken the easy way out at the time, I would have missed this blessing that God had for us. We all would have suffered in the long run. I am so thankful for my prayer partners, the 1st Peter 3 girls and others, who encouraged me and upheld me in prayer to do the hard thing. The right thing! I praise God for the blessing! I praise God for teaching me to love again.

It has been a long road and I am aware that it still will be. I am thankful for what I have learned. Romans 8:28 means much more to me now. Many people say that something good will come out of every situation that God brings our way. I never wanted to believe it, but now I have *seen* it!

JULIA

I became involved with the 1st Peter 3 girls at a turning point in my life. Before my husband and I were married and up until after we had our second child, we were once a week churchgoers attending a local Catholic church. Then my husband was invited to attend a Promise Keepers Conference and our lives have never been the same. He had made a personal commitment to Jesus Christ and after sharing his newfound faith with me, I too committed my life to Jesus. Kent began to deepen his relationship with the Lord and has become the strong spiritual leader that he is called to be.

I, however, had come to a point in my life where I needed to make some decisions. I had just become pregnant with our fourth child and we were debating whether or not I should quit my part-time job and become full-time, stay-at-home mom. Up until this point Kent and I had not been seriously challenged in our faith and we were about to be tested. I had always worked pretty much at least two or three days a week since shortly after I had my first child and the prospect of being home with four children ranging in age from newborn to 7 was quite overwhelming to me.

The two older children were becoming quite active in extracurricular activities and I was having a difficult time getting them to and from everything on time even working only a few days a week. I felt torn between work and my need to be there for my children. I felt I was cheating both and running myself ragged. I tend to be a perfectionist and I was feeling my performance in both areas was definitely less than perfect and it really bothered me. Kent had been traveling quite a bit with his job so the responsibility fell mostly to me. He could see and feel the tension that this stress was causing and he initially suggested that I quit. At first I was totally against the idea, thinking that my patience could not bear being home with the children all day long and that they were much better off at the sitters. In addition we had just moved into a new home in a nice subdivision and we certainly could not afford for me to quit working. But God had a different plan in mind for me and He began to soften my heart.

It was during this time that I began to develop a closer relationship with my friend, Maggie, at work. We had talked about our faith, our families, and many other things. She introduced me to The 1st Peter 3 girls and asked me if I would like to join them. These women immediately accepted me into their group and I began to communicate all of the issues I was dealing with in my life. They prayed for me and encouraged me to seek God's will and to follow His calling. Since my husband was eager for me to be at home, they encouraged me to trust God in this area and follow my husband's wishes. They are so good to me. They gave me scripture to refer to and guided me. They spoke from the heart and from their own experiences. To make this long story short, I did finally decide to quit my job about a month before the baby was born. Just before my last day on the job, my wonderful husband arranged for my family and friends to send me cards and letters of encouragement to support me in my decision. I will never forget my last day of work. I returned home after a very emotional day, Kent sat me on the couch and presented me with all of the cards, letters, and email messages that he had been collecting. I sat on there and cried tears of joy and relief as I had finally committed to our decision. Each one of my 1st Peter 3 sisters had sent something and it meant the world to me.

During the next few months God would confirm this decision in our lives. We were to face another test after the birth of Andrew, our son. Almost immediately after we brought him home from the hospital, we noticed that he didn't appear to startle or respond like a newborn should to noise. And believe me there were many people and noises in our home to be startled by with the six of us. We took him in for testing at 5 weeks and our worst fears were confirmed. He appeared to have a significant loss of hearing. After the initial shock and grief, we got on our knees and sent out prayer requests to family, friends, and of course, my 1st Peter 3 sisters. They were mothers. They could relate to what I was feeling.

It would be months before they could run tests that would determine the extent of the hearing loss and I have to tell you that those months were some of the longest months in my life. Andrew was almost 5 months old when that test took place. The 1st Peter 3 girls prayed and fasted along with us on that scary but glorious day as we sat in amazement in the technicians office as she performed the tests and Andrew scored perfectly in all ranges and pitches. It was a miracle and we witnessed it right before our eyes. Thanks to the wonderful grace of God and the faithful prayers of our friends and family, Andrew could hear!

I certainly have not been faced with the major challenges that most of the women in our group have been faced with. Nor was I brought up in a Christ centered, Bible teaching home, but I am learning and growing in my walk daily and hope to be able to give back to these women and others as much as they have given to me. I have acquired the official title of 'cheerleader' of the group and it seems to fit. I pray that I can be that and much more to them in the future.

Although I do not regret my decision to be a full-time, at-home mom, I still struggle with it at times. I have had my own issues to deal with such as the time and energy to have an intimate relationship with my husband, and then the emotional strain in losing my mother to cancer. But in each of these situations these women have been there for me to listen, to give me sound biblical guidance, support and encourage me, and most of all, to pray for me. They are all a true blessing to me and I look forward to continuing to grow and learn together as we strive to be all God has called us to be.

STACY

I have really learned so much from this whole situation with our prodigal daughter. It has been a real growing process for both Greg and I and we couldn't have made it without having Jesus Christ as our personal savior. We still have our bad days, but I think the biggest lesson has been to trust God and really put our faith in Him knowing that He knows the big picture and we don't. We like to think we are in control but its when things like these that come into our lives that we have realized that God wants control and wants us to relinquish our control over to Him. I praise God everyday for my special 1Peter sisters in the Lord, they have stood by me with so much encouragement through the past couple of years. It has been a real blessing to have them in my life and to know that they will say it like it is and not just pacify me. I love every one of them and each one brings a different perspective and gift to this group. Praise God that they have been there in my time of need!

MAGGIE

I can't even begin to describe to you how important this support system has been to me. It was so awesome having other Christian women pointing to Christ and holding me up when I felt like going limp. It has been my lifeline. So many times, in my devastation I felt very alone. I had absolutely no support from anyone regarding working on my marriage. My husband loved another woman. I was told, "There's a point in a bad marriage where there's no turning back. Why would you still want to be married to him?" I often wondered, 'was I so insecure that I would cling to my husband and stay married when he didn't want me?'

Don't buy Satan's lies. Love is a choice. To not love your spouse is a sin. And God has already proven he is BIGGER than sin. As has been described in this book, I am by nature a very strong woman. I will NOT be a door mat for anyone. But through seeking God's will I determined that if God wanted me to be what seemed like a "door mat" then so be it. Weak women don't stay in bad marriages and seek to live God's will. STRONG WOMEN DO!

Matthew 19:26 "Jesus looked at them and said, 'With man this is impossible, but with God all things are possible'." NIV

Divorce is not God's plan for us. God can do anything, change anything. Beauty for ashes. Strength for fear. We can become the very creatures God created us to be by obeying His Word. My God is the God of the impossible. It has been such a blessing for me to see how far my husband and I have come. We are truly different people. We don't have the marriage we had years ago. I know in my heart I would have truly missed God's blessing had I left my marriage for someone who I thought could love me. I am truly thankful for this group of women who God has used to help restore my life and guide me in the right direction. I am also grateful for my forgiving, loving God, who cared enough about me to get my attention in order to have a much fuller, richer relationship with Him.

LORI

The 1st Peter 3 girls have been a great support and encouragement to me. Discipling me in my growing relationship with Jesus. It was a BIG job. The group shared the burden. Someone from the group is usually able to respond when a concern is voiced and we can take turns as GOD leads us—sharing the emotional and time consuming burden of listening to, empathizing with, giving advice and praying for each other.

When women are discouraged we need help. This society does not offer a lot of truly biblical help. Even Christian counselors can give you an 'out' for divorce (except for one counselor we went to, Dave —thanks Dave). Christian women don't need an out. We need to hear that God does miracles today. We need to vent our feelings and then be told to hang on to God's word and pray. We need to believe that God is big enough to do anything and that God cares enough to do it. We need friends who will confront us with our flaws and help us to change. We need accountability. We need patience. We need to love and trust God whatever the outcome. We need support to walk through our troubles because Jesus died on a cross for us. He loved us enough to die for us.

Yes, it is painful, but not as painful as what Jesus did for each of us.

We all need friends to quote us scripture like— *Matthew 19:26*

Jesus looked at them and said, "With man this is impossible, but with God all things are possible." NIV

And,

Psalm 77:14 "You are the God who performs miracles; you display your power among the peoples." NIV

I did not journal during the bad times. I just wanted to survive day by day and not ever look back. I am more inclined to write now about what God has done. It is a visible miracle.

The change in Dan has been truly unbelievable. I was so skeptical in the beginning. I didn't want to hope for real change and then be hurt again. But this change was **REAL**. The people who really know him saw it. I saw it, the kids' saw it and our close friends saw it. *God* changed Dan's heart. Dan only had to surrender his will to God's will.

Dan started to talk about a joy he felt that he never had before. He looked happy. He started to get frustrated with superficial relationships. He wanted honesty and meaning in his relationships.

God brought a childhood friend back into Dan's life and it quickly came out that they shared more than they ever knew. An addiction to pornography. Dan was put into the position of discipling this other man and it has been a huge growing experience for him.

Dan cared more than ever about his relationship with me and with the kids. I saw the kids starting to love their dad more and enjoy his company. Dan started to see the frustration that he had put us through with his deceptions. He longed for more meaning and honesty in his relationship with his parents and sibling. He strove to care about others more and to show it. When he would slip back into his pattern of procrastination and laziness, he would more quickly see it and correct the problem.

Then, a few months ago, Dan said that he felt God calling him to apply for a ministry position out of town. I could see that God was speaking to Dan. And, more importantly, that Dan was listening. The job is unrelated to what his degree is in and it would require a major change in our lives, but Dan quickly acted on what he felt God was leading him to do and obeyed God. We have not heard anything as of yet, but we are waiting to see how God is going to work this situation out in our lives. We are willing to obey and go where God sends us.

I love my 1 peter 3 sisters. They have been here with me and witnessed this awesome miracle. They are the kind of friends who point me in the direction of God. They lift me up and encourage me and I have been truly blessed to be a part of this group.

A FEW WORDS FROM DAN

Marlene had asked me to write something for the 1st Peter 3 Girls book and after some thought and prayer, I said "O.K". I would write something. But what? What did I really want to say? What did God want me to say? I wanted to read the book first, and then I might know what to say. She was afraid to let me read it you know. She thought that maybe I might get angry.

As I was reading what she had written, I wanted to say, "Wait a minute! That's not me!" But then I would think, 'Yes, that *was* me'. Each time I would read something she had written about me, I would want to say, "Yeah, but what about this?" or, "What about that?" She was writing from her perspective and as I was reading I wanted to give the "reasons" for the way I had acted. For instance, I wanted to tell the part about when I was young, probably eight years old, when the older neighbor boy approached me and did things that were inappropriate. Or the time in sixth grade, when another boy my age approached me and we also did things that were inappropriate. Or, how about my family? A good loving family from all appearances. A Christian home, but no one talked about important stuff. Only about how things should look on the outside.

You see I could blame many things, many people, and I did. I even blamed God. Because God could remove these thoughts and feelings if He wanted to, and believe me I asked Him many times. But I had taken some things that happened to me and nurtured them for years and years and years. I thought getting married would solve my problems, but that only compounded them. I felt relieved when I had finally spilled my story. But I didn't want to change. I *said* I did, and believe me, I tried to change, but in my own strength. It didn't work. I would go through the motions, and then I would let my feelings get in the way. I wouldn't *feel* like doing this or that.

I guess what I am trying to say, is that we all have a choice. Sometime it seems clearer than others. The choice is to submit our will to God. See this is what

Marlene is talking about in this book. How these ladies made a conscious choice to submit their will, their desires, their hopes and dreams to God. Lori had gotten lots of counsel. Some wise, and most of it was well intended but not very godly. From a pastor's wife to "Christian" counselors she was told to take the kids and leave me. After all, she did have biblical grounds. But there was this 1st Peter 3 group who encouraged her when she needed it. Sometimes she would tell me what they would say in an effort to get me to change, but I would say, "They only know your half of the story." *Surely* she was tainting the picture in her favor. If they only knew the whole story, they would see it my way, I thought. Everyone else had it all wrong, at least from my perspective. From hindsight, I praise God that Lori had the 1st Peter3 girls for support. I think without them, she would have taken the other advice and left me long ago.

I put Lori through a lot of pain...much more than I may ever know and understand. I can see that Lori is a woman who wants to please God, truly a woman after God's heart. God truly worked a miracle in our lives and he took care of the rest of the story. In my life it wasn't about homosexuality, it was about doing what was right in God's eyes in submitting my will to His.

Deceiving; that is what my life had been all about. Making people think that everything was "OK" when it really wasn't. I would go to church, sing in the choir, be on the praise team, play the piano, etc. I thought I was fooling everyone, but I was the one who was the fool. And then, one day, God asked me to walk down the isle at church and tell everyone that I was pretending. How could I do that? I had done such a great job of pretending, what would people think? Pride. Wow, what a stumbling block.

It really is a simple choice, to submit our will to God's. The choice is simple, but the work and the cost seems at times too much to bear. However, since I've submitted my life, my will unto God, I have known a joy that I did not know before.

Do I struggle with old feelings and habits? Absolutely, yes. But God is bigger than all of my struggles and he has done, and continues to do, a good work in me as long as I submit to Him. *Philippians 1:6 "being confident of this, that he who began a good work in you will carry it on to completion until the day of Christ Jesus." NIV*- I really believe this, and I think if you look at verse 5, it really is a choice. Verse 5 says" because of your partnership...". If we don't submit our wills in partnership with God, then we are the losers. And we can question in all of our circumstances...where is God? But He never leaves us. God created us for fellowship with Him, but he loved us enough to give us a choice, a free will.

I would just close with a verse that is special to me. *Romans 5:38* tells us that *"...neither death nor life, neither angels nor demons, neither the present nor the future, nor any powers, neither height nor depth, not anything else in all creation, will be able to separate us from the love of God that is in Christ Jesus our Lord." NIV*

So what will be your choice?

God is so *awesome.* I get overwhelmed just reading back through what Dan and the girls have shared with you. Based upon the evidence you have read in these pages, let me answer the questions for you that I have asked repeatedly.

YES, God *is* who He says He is and, **YES** His Word *is* True! Believe it! Accept it! Live it! And then reap the unspeakable blessings of an intimate relationship with the God who loves you and wants to heal your hurts. The 1st Peter 3 girls have and we wanted to share it with you. We also want to challenge you, as a woman, to find out what it means in your own life to be a 1st Peter 3 girl according to God's Word and then to pass the legacy on.

CHAPTER TWENTY THREE

Pass On A Legacy

So let's boil this down. What does it mean to be a "1st Peter 3 girl"?

As a child of God I must be committed to obeying God's Word and applying it in my daily walk. Every role I fill must be done "as unto the Lord". As a wife I must be committed to my husband and the role that God has called me to. As a mother, my first responsibility of discipleship is to my children. They are a gift from God and I am instructed to bring them up in the nurture and admonition of the Lord. But I am also called, as a believer, to go and make disciples in my world. And even more specifically, as a woman, I am told that I am to participate in the Body of Christ by also teaching and instructing younger women and sisters in Christ, in the ways of the Lord. Teaching and challenging them to a high calling in Christ Jesus. We are to spur each other on, to move forward together.

The 1st Peter 3 concept is not a new one. It is a Biblical one. God is the author and commands us to participate in the Body of Christ, using the gifts he has divinely blessed us with in our relationships. We have simply put a name to our particular method and organized practical application. The message is as it has always been; God saves and transforms lives. We simply are committed to sharing that and encouraging each other to press on toward the goal.

As we have shared our individual lives and testimonies with other women and as I have had opportunity to speak to groups on occasion, questions have been asked about the group and how we have organized and if there are guidelines that we follow. As we began to add to our accountability group, one by one, we realized we needed to set some boundaries in place to keep us focused and on track. Let me share with you our commitment and the guidelines we set up for ourselves and how it has worked for us.

Here is what we came up with:

WE AGREE:

- That the purpose of the 1st Peter 3 group was for the developing of intimate female relationships that encourage and edify us as sisters in Christ and to hold each other personally accountable in our daily walk with Jesus.

- That as we became more intimate in our sharing, we would keep information shared within the group or to extend only to spouses (if appropriate). This would ensure each persons' privacy and gives that person freedom to share sensitive issues and gives the others freedom to respond in an uplifting, biblical manner.

- That we are each free to *vent* but not *bash* – this includes personal attacks directed toward spouses, friends, co-workers, relatives, and each other – freedom to vent enables us to be real and honest with our feelings and yet vulnerable to each other so we can confront in love, encourage, admonish, forgive, work through, and grow together.

- That we would limit the number of individuals in the group because, as an accountability group, we will have a greater impact on each other in a smaller more intimate setting and to also ensure the privacy of each woman
- To hold each other up in prayer and to fast together
- To limit our prayer requests to individuals in the group or immediate family and to situations that relate to each person in a way that we can keep track of and understand as we get to know that person.
- To work on memorization of scripture – Psalm 119:11
- Understanding and allowing for the fact that we each have busy schedules, we agreed to not neglect our commitment to one another when we are needed – we all have times when we are needier or busier than others and we need to be able to count on each other as time and our families allow.

These are the basics of our commitment to each other as the 1st Peter 3 girls. This is the basic framework that sets up the dynamics of our group. We have committed to being guardrails for each other. When we get off track the guard rails let us know we are headed in a dangerous direction. Sometimes you actually run into a guardrail and you and the guardrail get a little mangled but it may save a life.

As for the practical application of the 1st Peter 3 principles we have been learning, we have spent much time praying and directing our attention to our own wrong patterns in our marriage relationships. We have dealt often with the submission issue and what it means and doesn't mean in each of our individual situations. We have spent time trying to pin point our tendencies toward manipulation and control. We have dealt with identifying false guilt and enabling patterns. We have even tackled the sex issue and our tendencies to not meet the needs of our spouses in this area. And of course, one of the critical issues we each have faced continually is when to SHUT UP and let our husbands take responsibility for their own choices and behavior. Only with the power of the Holy Spirit and prayer are we able to effectively deal with and change these patterns in our lives as women. God has been loving and gracious enough to give us each other to sharpen, challenge and come along side for support.

We have also had great times of fellowship together in person. We initially saw a need to get together face to face after our group had grown and so many of us had not actually met. After our first meeting we had such a great time talking and sharing together we decided to make it a priority every several months. Sometimes it's just for a few hours over dinner, or at one of the girl's houses sitting in a hot tub laughing and just being women. Occasionally we try to all meet at a hotel for an overnighter, which turns into an all night sharing and prayer session. Its not always easy since some of us live out of state but we plan and see it as important in making the concept work. The in-person times are a must for connecting as believers. It helps to remove the impersonal distance and misunderstandings that sometimes accompany email communication. It also establishes better communication and accountability when we've met face to face. We are not just words on a computer screen, we are human beings and it is so easy to lose sight of that in this age of technology when, with the click of the delete button, we can erase a person's identity from our screen. Talking face to face strengthens our commitment to each other and deepens our relationships. Besides it can be just plain old fun. A time when the joy of the Lord rings loudly and it certainly does with our group.

A WORD OF CAUTION

We are all, as believers, sinners saved by grace and we are all at different places in our walk with the Lord and to become involved in such a commitment means to be willing to have patience with each other. This may mean disagreements and dealing with a weaker sister at times. We all come with baggage of some sort and different issues but we humbly press on together.

Phil 3:12-14 "Not that I have already obtained all this, or have already been made perfect, but I press on to take hold of that for which Christ Jesus took hold of me. Brothers (sisters) I do not consider myself yet to have taken hold of it. But one thing I do: forgetting what is behind and straining toward what is ahead, I press on toward the goal to win the prize for which God has called me heavenward in Christ Jesus." NIV

The bottom line should *always* be God's Word and pressing on toward maturity together. Dig, dig, and dig in the Word. Hold each other to it. Encourage each other with it. Love each other as it says to.

For an accountability group to really be effective it should include at least one or more spiritually mature

Christian woman who can be trusted to keep things on track and can rightly divide God's Word and direct others to it. There may be times when a mediator is needed between group members who disagree. To work through these times is to mature and grow in grace and the knowledge of our Lord. I have wept at times over and with these women. I have hurt for them. I have been on my face before God with them. And through it all God has grown me along with my sisters. As we develop Godly disciplines as women, we begin to get a glimpse of how big our God really is.

We also need to caution ourselves, as women, to make sure that any group or organization, even church responsibility, does not take away from our responsibilities and relationships at home. We cannot afford to live vicariously through the lives of others or with a sense of self-importance as if *we* are the only ones who can help individuals. The relationships we cultivate in an accountability group should *enhance* our roles as wives, and not become a substitute or priority over our God given roles and relationships in our families. We need to be building up each other's marriages, not spending time husband bashing or so busy "being there" for, and helping, others that our own families suffer. God has solutions, not band aides and if it doesn't play out in your own life at home, you cannot be a true help to others. I cannot ask anyone to obey God's Word if I am not willing to do so myself.

I pray that I can walk before my own daughter in a manner worthy of the calling of mother. I want to pass on the 1st Peter 3 legacy. I want to teach her what it is to walk in wisdom. To exercise discernment. To not just live unto herself but reach out to her friends and

171

her sisters in Christ. To know what the Bible means by quiet and gentle spirit. I want her to feel the passion for a God who is passionate about her. I pray that, as she grows, God brings into her life other girls and women committed to being God's women; to hold her up in prayer and challenge her in her walk. And I pray that God gives me the wisdom as a mother to raise a 1st Peter 3 girl who will honor her God and her husband and will pass the legacy on to her own daughter some day.

I pray that no matter what circumstances you find yourself in, that you have found within these pages the redeeming message of God's love and grace and the hope that He has brought to these women. And I challenge *you* to become a 1st Peter 3 girl and then pass the legacy on.

About The Author

Marlene Lawson has been involved in active Christian ministry for over 23 years. Most recently she has worked with various women's ministries as a speaker and seminar leader. as well as developing the 1st Peter 3 Girls Ministry working with women in crisis. She also is a frequent speaker for local MOPS programs and brings her own unique brand of humor to her presentations. Married and the mother of two children, Marlene lists her credentials as, PhaDE – "Professional Homemaker and Domestic Engineer", believing that two of the most significant and influential roles a woman can choose to fill is that of wife and mother.

Printed in the United States
21455LVS00002B/79-96